The Process of Unbecoming

A Different Relationship to Being Human

Lacey K. Kelly, LCSW

Unbecoming You, LLC

For the Great Mystery—

the ever-evolving experience that is life

and the unknown that humbly reminds me

that nothing is ever guaranteed.

To my mother,

who taught me to protect my sense of wonder

and to stay open to life's experiences even when they are difficult.

To Lauren,

who inspires creativity and depth in my soul.

To Kyli,

who helps me keep one foot in the ether

and one on the earth.

To my wonderful husband, Jake,

who believes in me

even when I forget how to believe in myself.

And to my miracle son, Auden,

who has shown me that the real magic lies in being human.

Contents

A Note From the Author

I have felt an ache for as long as I can remember. It was not subtle or passing, and it was not something I could set down. It arrived early and stayed — a constant sense that something was wrong and that life was slightly misaligned. I was living inside a question I could not answer or escape.

I looked outward first. My childhood had its difficulties, but nothing that explained the depth or persistence of what I carried. On the outside, things were fine. Inside, I was never settled. The ache did not come and go. It organized my life.

Eventually, I turned inward, convinced there had to be a way to fix it. I started practicing yoga when I was twelve. I remember the relief of believing there might finally be an answer — not just calm or coping, but an actual solution and a way out of the feeling. I threw myself into it with the hope that discipline, insight, or transcendence would resolve whatever was wrong with me. Years later, I would understand this as spiritual bypassing. At the time, it felt like survival. I was not learning how to be human. I was trying to outrun my humanness entirely.

When that did not work, I turned to everything else that promised relief — therapy, medications, spiritual retreats, psychedelic experiences — each one carried the same desperate hope that this would be the thing. When none of it worked, the only conclusion that made sense was that I was broken, somehow exempt from relief, and destined to live with a sense of lack.

What made this harder to explain was that my life looked successful. I was teaching yoga and working as a yoga therapist. By the time I was twenty-one, I owned and operated two studios. I was living my dream and pursuing my passion. I loved my work. I was good at it. And still, the ache did not relent.

Eventually, I collapsed under the weight of the effort — not the effort of working or caring for others, which I could sustain, but the effort of trying to understand myself, of trying to fix whatever was wrong. I sold the studios and stopped. I wandered and waited, assuming the exhaustion had come from working too much.

It had not. Slowing down did not touch the ache. Changing my life did not touch it. Nothing touched it.

Needing some kind of ground again, I decided to go back to school to become a clinician. At the time, it felt like failure. It was not what I wanted, and it felt like surrendering to a conventional life I believed would make me miserable. I hated school. And still, it made sense given my lifelong role as the peacekeeper, my obsession with understanding people, and my tendency to see patterns everywhere.

A few months into graduate school, I was diagnosed with an autoimmune disorder that affected my skin and muscles. Until then, my life had been deeply physical. The diagnosis took all of that away. I was forced inside, forced to stop, and forced to think in a way I had not allowed myself to before.

The autoimmune world is saturated with blame. It tells you that you caused this — unresolved trauma, poor boundaries, stress, diet, something you did led to this. And if you caused it, you can fix it. The message is relentless: this is your fault, and therefore your responsibility to undo.

I was furious. And of course, I tried to fix it.

That only intensified the effort, the self-rejection, and the confusion. How could someone who meditated, taught yoga, moved her body, and cared deeply about her health end up with a disorder that implied she was too stressed, too unresolved, too broken — so much so that her body had turned against itself? It did not make sense, so I returned to diagnosing myself. Depression. Anxiety. OCD. Trauma. Poor boundaries. Overtraining. Each explanation landed in the same place: there is something wrong with you. And I had an entire culture, entire fields of study, ready to confirm it.

Eventually, I stopped looking for the right diagnosis. I sat. I thought. Mostly about the question I had been living with since childhood: what does it actually mean to be human?

What I began to see was that I had been living in a world organized around becoming. Become your vocation. Become your roles. Become regulated. Become healed. Become spiritual. Become something other than human. And alongside that, a constant demand to fight the human condition itself — sadness, grief, apathy, vulnerability, the body. The promise was everywhere and seldom questioned: become the right thing, eliminate the wrong parts, and life will hurt less.

It was exhausting.

And then I sat with it from the other side of the room.

As a clinician, I watched people struggle with ordinary human experiences and conclude they were broken because of them. I watched them work hard, stay committed, and still feel like they were not getting there. And there I was, expected to diagnose the problem, to name what was wrong, and in doing so, reinforce the same story that had nearly emptied my own life of meaning.

I could not do it.

What I had been living — and what I kept witnessing in the people I worked with — was not a failure of effort or insight. It was the cost of a premise that had never been examined. The premise that something essential was missing. That being human, as we are, is not enough yet.

The work that actually moved something was not the work of becoming. It was the work of unbecoming — of setting down the accumulated weight of who we had learned to be, so that what was always already present could be felt again.

I am not writing from a place of arrival. I am still affected by life, still shaped by relationships and circumstances, and still human. What shifted was not that I found the right answers. It was that I stopped directing my life around the belief that I was incomplete.

This book is an invitation to stand on different ground — one that does not require becoming someone else in order to feel at ease, connected, or at home in your own life.

Welcome to *The Process of Unbecoming*.

Introduction

You are a human.

That means something. It is easy to forget — not because the truth is subtle, but because the world is loud. We live in a culture that does not know how to hold human life as it is being lived. A culture that offers improvement in place of meaning, explanation in place of contact, and control in place of relationship. Much of what makes us human has nowhere to go.

And yet, everything we need in order to be here already exists. Death clarifies what matters by taking it. Birth reminds us that life arrives whole, without having to earn its place. The seasons show us that nothing stays fixed. Grief exposes the depth of love. These are not metaphors. They are conditions of being alive.

We forget this. The forgetting is not mild. It produces a sense of wrongness, a restlessness, a persistent feeling that life should feel more inhabitable than it does. Not necessarily easier, but more grounded. Less effortful. Less managed. And when there is no shared frame to hold the human condition, that unease turns inward — and the culture is ready for it.

Become regulated. Become healed. Become your best self. Become the version of you that has done the work, processed the trauma, rewired the nervous system, and arrived at the life you were always meant to live. The message is everywhere — in therapy offices, in wellness culture, in the language of personal development, in the pressure of social media feeds that make it look like everyone else is further along than you are. The promise is consistent: if you just understand yourself deeply enough, apply the right framework, and stay committed to the process, you will eventually get there.

Most of us have tried. Many of us have tried for years.

We have done the therapy. We have read the books, attended the retreats, downloaded the apps, and built the morning routines. We have learned to name our attachment styles, identify our nervous system states, and recognize our patterns. Some of it has helped. And still, for so many people, there is a persistent sense that they are not quite there yet — that something essential is still missing, still unresolved, still in need of correction. The insight lands, the relief is real, and then life continues, and the old weight returns. So we go back. We try harder. We find the next thing.

This is not a failure of effort. It is the predictable outcome of a premise that was never examined.

The premise is this: that something is fundamentally wrong with you, and that the work of your life is to fix it. That you are, at your core, incomplete — and that the goal is to become complete. This premise is so embedded in how we talk about mental health, growth, and healing that it rarely gets questioned. It just gets assumed. And from that assumption, an entire industry has been built — one that profits from the belief that you are not yet enough, and that the right product, practice, or professional can finally get you there.

The problem is not that these tools don't work. Some of them do, in real and meaningful ways. The problem is that they are all operating within the same paradigm.

They are all, at their root, trying to help you become something other than what you already are. And when you are working from the premise that you are broken, no amount of fixing will ever feel like enough. You will always find the next thing that needs repair, because the premise itself demands it.

What I kept witnessing — in my own life and in the lives of the people I work with as a clinician — was not a failure of effort or insight. It was the cost of this unexamined premise. People who had done years of work, who were genuinely committed and genuinely self-aware, still carried the same ache. Still measuring themselves against an idealized version of themselves that kept moving just out of reach. Still treating their own lives as evidence of how far they had yet to go.

There is a kind of exhaustion that comes from this. It is not the exhaustion of working hard or caring deeply. It is the exhaustion of never arriving. Of living inside a framework that keeps promising relief and keeps deferring it. Of being human — messy, fluctuating, contradictory, and alive — in a world that treats all of that as a problem to be solved.

Unbecoming is a different premise entirely.

It does not offer a better method for becoming. It does not promise that if you follow these steps, you will finally feel okay. What it offers is a different starting point — one that asks: what if you were never broken to begin with? What if the wholeness you have been searching for is not something you have to earn, restore, or achieve, but something already present in the simple fact of being human?

Being human already includes everything you need to navigate being human. Not in a motivational sense — not as a reminder that you are capable or resilient or strong.

But in a more fundamental sense: the capacity to meet experience, to be affected, to recover, to connect, to feel, to lose, to continue — this is not something you have to develop. It is what you already are. What gets in the way is not a lack of capacity, but the accumulated weight of learning to distrust it.

Unbecoming is the process of setting that weight down and loosening the grip of who you have learned to be — the roles, the adaptations, the stories about what is wrong with you — so that what has always been present can be felt again.

How This Book Is Organized

This book is organized into four main sections, separated by two shorter bridges.

The Ground lays the foundation, offering a set of principles that form a different premise for understanding what it means to be human.

Interlude: The First and Last Teacher steps outside the framework to synthesize those principles through the lived experiences of birth and death.

What Begins to Shift explores what naturally reorganizes in the background when that foundation changes. In Motion is a short personal story that bridges what shifts in the background and what it looks like in the foreground of a life.

The Phases maps the recurring movements that tend to accompany this process — Awareness, Unraveling, Emerging, Animating, and Returning.

Returning to the Phases offers companionship for the return — because this is not a linear process, and there will be times when the ground feels less steady.

You do not have to move through this book in order. You do not have to agree with everything in it to find something useful. You only have to be willing to consider that the premise you have been working from might not be the only one available.

From here, we begin by laying the ground.

The Ground

B efore experience shapes us, before conditioning layers over us, before we learn what we are supposed
to want and who we are supposed to be — something is
already here.

A human being arrives with the capacity to feel, to connect, to be moved, to recover, to make meaning, to sense
what is true. These are not achievements. They are not
things we develop through the right practices or accumulate through enough insight. They are the original
equipment of being alive. The capacity to be affected by
what happens. The capacity to return to ourselves after
being pulled away. The capacity to be in relationship —
with other people, with experience, with the world as it
actually is.

This is what the principles in this section are grounded
in. Not in what we need to become, but in what is already
present by nature of being human.

The principles are not instructions. They do not ask you
to do anything differently or believe anything on faith.
They are more like a different set of glasses — a way of
looking at human experience that starts from what is inherent rather than what is lacking. When you read them,
you may find that they name something you have always
sensed but never had language for. Or you may find them
difficult to hold, because the premise of brokenness has
been present for so long that wholeness feels abstract or

unconvincing. Both responses are fine. You do not have to feel the principles to consider them. The rest of the book is what gives them ground.

What changes when these principles are assumed as the starting point is not that life becomes easier or that difficulty disappears. What changes is the relationship to difficulty. When wholeness is the ground rather than the goal, experience stops being evidence of how far you have yet to go. It becomes something you can actually be in — something you can meet, feel, and move through.

Chapter 1

Wholeness is Inherent

There is something essential about human life that remains intact regardless of experience. Wholeness, as it is used here, does not describe how life feels or how well things are going. It affirms that a human life exists as a whole by virtue of its existence. It is present from the beginning and neither added by development nor removed by harm. It exists prior to identity, personality, and the ways we learn to adapt in order to belong, stay safe, or be loved. This is not something a person grows into. It is a condition of being human.

Most of us, however, do not live as though this is true. The premise many people carry into adulthood is that something essential is missing—that we are not quite enough, not healed enough, not regulated enough, not far enough along. It shows up as a low hum beneath ordinary life, a sense that we are always a little behind where we should be and that something important still needs to be fixed or completed before we can finally feel at ease.

This principle offers a different starting point.

Wholeness is not a destination, nor a state you arrive at after enough healing or work. It is the essential nature you were born with, and it has never left.

Inside that nature live the qualities that make a human being human: the vulnerability that allows you to be moved, the capacity to feel and respond to the world, the pull toward connection, the longing to be known and to belong. The part of you that reaches for others, that dreams, that loves, that aches when connection is lost. These are not weaknesses or signs of deficiency. They are conditions of being alive.

This is the soft interior—the tender place that, when unarmored, is where you are most fully yourself. It exists underneath the roles, the performances, and the adaptations you developed in order to navigate life. It is the part that has been there the whole time.

That is what wholeness names: not an abstract state of perfection, but the living interior that is yours by nature of being human.

This became clearest to me when my son was born. I remember looking into his eyes and being stopped by what was there. It was not innocence in a sentimental sense, nor potential waiting to unfold. It felt like pure life looking back at me, whole and unmistakably present.

There was no sense of lack, no movement toward becoming something else. Nothing needed to be added. Nothing needed to arrive later. There was simply a human life there, fully itself, meeting mine.

The recognition did not come through thought. There was no evaluation, no comparison, no narrative about who he might become or what kind of life he would live—only the undeniable sense of wholeness contained in that moment of contact. Whatever he would go on to experience—joy, pain, confusion, love—could not undo what was already there. It was not fragile, and it did not depend on conditions.

That same wholeness does not belong only to the beginning of life. It is not tied to age, innocence, or dependency. What changes over time is not what is essential, but how attention becomes oriented.

As life unfolds, attention turns outward. Experience teaches us what is welcome, what carries risk, and what must be managed in order to stay connected to the people and environments that matter. Identity forms. Protection takes shape. Over time, we become increasingly focused on navigating, interpreting, and securing a place in the world.

As this happens, contact with that interior can become less reliable—not because it has disappeared, but because it is no longer where attention rests. Layers accumulate. Life leaves its mark. What is inherent remains intact, though it can become harder to feel beneath everything that has been added.

Wholeness does not disappear when life becomes complicated. It is not replaced by personality or erased by pain. A person can be deeply affected by experience without losing what is essential. Experience shapes and constrains a life, but it does not undo the fact of that life being here.

Sometimes this becomes visible in very simple moments.

I once sat with someone who described sitting in her car after a particularly difficult therapy session. She had spent the hour talking about all the ways she felt broken, all the patterns she needed to fix. She was exhausted.

Then, sitting in the parking lot, she noticed something very ordinary. She was breathing. Her heart was beating. Her body was doing what it needed to do to keep her alive, without her having to manage it or earn it.

For just a moment, she felt the simple fact of being intact underneath all the brokenness she had been describing—not the capable or high-functioning version of herself, but the one underneath that. The one that was simply alive, present, here.

It did not fix anything. It did not resolve the patterns or remove the pain. But it was there—whole and unchanged by everything she had been carrying.

Holding wholeness as inherent does not remove difficulty. Pain is still pain. Hard things are still hard. What changes is how difficulty is understood. It stops being evidence that something essential is wrong with you. It becomes something that happens within a life that remains whole.

Over time, this understanding can subtly reorganize how life is met. The impulse to fix, improve, or prove yourself may soften as the assumption of incompleteness loosens its grip. Wholeness shifts from something you are trying to achieve into something that quietly exists in the background.

Attention will drift. There will be days when that interior feels distant or buried beneath the conditions of life. That is not a failure. It is part of being human.

What matters is that it remains.

You were born with it. You will die with it.

Everything that happens in between takes place within a life that was already whole.

Chapter 2

Identity is Adaptive

When the premise is that something is wrong with you, identity easily becomes evidence. Every role you play, every pattern you repeat, every way you learned to move through the world can begin to look like proof of damage—something to diagnose, dismantle, or fix. The self becomes a problem to solve.

This principle offers a different framing.

Adaptation is not a mistake or a deviation from wholeness. It is a feature of the human condition itself.

You were built to adapt. Your nervous system, your psychology, and your capacity for relationship are all designed to read the environment and adjust. This is not a vulnerability but one of the most sophisticated capacities of being human. It is how we survive, how we belong, and how we find our way in conditions we did not choose and cannot fully control.

For most of human history, the environments we adapted to were largely physical. Survival depended on reading the landscape, the weather, and the presence of threat. The adaptations were visible—behaviors and strategies that kept the body alive.

For many of us now, the environments we adapt to most are not physical. Our basic needs are largely met. The environments shaping us are emotional and relational: the need to belong, to be accepted, and to remain connected to the people who matter.

And these adaptations are harder to see. They do not live primarily in our behavior toward the external world. They live inside us—in the ways we learned to be, the parts we brought forward and the parts we kept back, the version of ourselves we offered to the people around us.

Identity forms in that space.

From the earliest moments of life, you were taking in information about the environment around you—what was welcomed, what created distance, what made connection feel safer or more uncertain—and adjusting accordingly.

This turning away is rarely deliberate. It happens gradually through repeated adjustments as attention shifts and expression narrows. What once felt natural can begin to feel risky, and maintaining connection may require some distance from parts of ourselves.

The ways you learned to be were not mistakes. They were resourceful responses to real conditions.

There is ingenuity in adaptation—the ability to read the environment and find a way to meet its demands. The role that made you more reliable, more helpful, more contained, or easier to be around formed because it worked. It stabilized belonging. It kept things from falling apart.

In one way or another, it answered a question every human being is always asking:

How do I stay connected here?

That is not damage. It is resourcefulness.

Difficulty arises when adaptations become so familiar, so automatic, and so woven into the texture of daily life that they stop feeling like adaptations. They begin to feel like you. The role that was once a strategy becomes identity. The way you learned to be begins to feel like the way you simply are.

"That's just how I am."

Most people recognize that phrase. It attaches to behaviors and tendencies that feel fixed—permanent features of the self rather than patterns that formed in response to conditions that may no longer exist.

Identity is not a fixed structure. It is a living, adaptive response that has crystallized into something that feels like fact.

I came to recognize this through the role I learned to inhabit as the responsible one.

Being capable, helpful, and steady made connection easier. It smoothed relationships, reduced uncertainty, and offered a sense of place. Over time, responsibility stopped feeling like something I did and began to feel like who I was.

The role made sense, but it also required a certain distance from myself. There was little room to need support, to feel unsure, or to let things unravel. Staying connected meant staying composed. Being helpful meant not being too affected.

What began as a way of preserving relationship gradually narrowed the range of what felt possible to express.

I did not choose that narrowing. It happened slowly, through the ordinary accumulation of adjustments that made belonging feel more secure. By the time I noticed it, it felt like personality.

This becomes clearer in everyday life.

A client once described how different she felt at work compared to at home. At work she was decisive, confident, and quick to speak up. At home with her partner she was hesitant, deferential, and quiet.

She had always interpreted this difference as inconsistency—as evidence that one version of her was not real.

But when she began to see identity as adaptive, something shifted. Both versions were real, and neither represented who she essentially was.

At work, the conditions called for decisiveness. At home, older patterns of protection made her small. The adaptations differed because the conditions did. What remained underneath did not.

When you begin to look at your own patterns through this lens, the view changes. Roles that once felt fixed become visible as responses. Behaviors that once carried shame can begin to make sense as adaptations to conditions that required them.

The question shifts.

Instead of asking, *Why am I like this?* You begin to ask, *What was this adaptation for?*

That question does not produce shame. It produces understanding.

And understanding loosens the grip of identity just enough to ask the next question: Does this adaptation still fit?

You are not your adaptations.

You are the one who adapted—resourcefully and intelligently, with what you had, in the conditions you were given. The adaptations are what you built, and what is built can be revisited, loosened, and eventually set down when the time is right.

Chapter 3

Capacity is Inherent

When the premise is that we are not capable, the logical response is to try to build capacity. We try to cultivate resilience, widen the window of tolerance, and train ourselves to become stronger, more regulated, more able to handle what life brings.

The effort is sincere. Yet it often produces more striving, more self-monitoring, and more distance from the very experience we are trying to meet. The work of becoming capable becomes another layer between us and ourselves.

This principle offers a different starting point.

Capacity is inherent.

Capacity names the human ability to meet experience at all—to register what is happening, to feel what is felt, and to respond from within experience rather than managing it from a distance. It is the ability to be affected by life and remain present enough for experience to move.

This capacity is not something we develop later. It is part of being human from the beginning.

If essential nature houses the qualities that make us human—the vulnerability, the need for connection, the impulse to feel and reach and respond—then capacity is the ability to express that nature. It is what essential nature looks like in motion.

Capacity is not a skill, and it is not something accumulated through enough practice or hardship. It is already present.

What changes over time is not the existence of capacity but our access to it.

Experience shapes how available capacity feels in a given moment. The ways we learn to protect ourselves—the distance we maintain from our own interior, the emotions we learn to manage or redirect—can affect how easily we meet what is happening. This does not mean capacity disappeared. It means the layers that formed around it can make contact more difficult.

Difficulty is often misread as incapacity.

When experience feels overwhelming—when emotion floods or shuts down, when the system contracts or goes quiet—it can appear as though something essential is missing. More often, these moments reflect load, timing, or the conditions surrounding the experience rather than the absence of capacity itself.

I saw this clearly the first time I taught yoga.

Standing in front of a room full of people, I felt exposed and unsteady. My heart raced. My thoughts scattered. I was certain I could not hold the room.

At one point my mentor said something simple: let the anxiety be in the room.

Nothing about the anxiety changed. It was still there—loud, physical, insistent. But my relationship to it shifted. I stopped structuring myself against it and allowed it to be present without trying to control it.

In that moment something became visible. I was already teaching. I was breathing, speaking, responding, aware of the people in front of me. The capacity I believed I lacked had been there all along. What changed was not its existence, but my access to it.

Capacity often reveals itself this way—through contact rather than readiness. It does not appear because we have finally prepared enough. It becomes visible when we stop bracing against experience and allow ourselves to be inside it.

A client once described something similar with her grief. For years she had kept a careful distance from it. She could feel it approaching and had learned to redirect herself before it arrived.

One afternoon, alone in her car after a difficult week, she stopped redirecting. She did not decide to cry. She simply did.

What she expected—the falling apart, the loss of control, the feeling that would be too much—did not come. The grief moved through her. She felt it fully, and she remained. Afterward she sat for a moment, started the car, and drove home.

Later she told me she had always assumed she could not handle it, that the management was necessary. What she discovered in that moment was that the capacity to hold her own grief had been there the whole time. She had simply never stopped bracing long enough to find it.

Seeing capacity this way changes how difficulty is understood. Struggle is no longer evidence of a gap that must be closed. It becomes information about what is happening in the moment—about timing, context, and what is being asked of the system right now.

The pressure to feel ready before acting begins to dissolve. Capacity does not require readiness. It requires presence.

Presence—the willingness to be inside your own experience rather than observing it from a distance—is not something you build. It is something you return to.

Essential nature houses the qualities that make you human. Capacity is what it looks like when those qualities are expressed.

It was always here, underneath the protection, waiting to be met.

Chapter 4

Protection Precedes Pathology

The premise that something is wrong with us often begins a search—the search to find the flaw and fix it. An entire culture is ready to support this effort. Diagnoses, frameworks, and self-help models frequently begin from the same starting point: that our patterns, reactions, and struggles are symptoms of something disordered or deficient that requires correction. The message is pervasive and often well-intentioned. Name what is broken, then work to repair it.

Yet this approach, however compassionate its intent, can reinforce the very premise it hopes to resolve. We become skilled at identifying what is wrong with us. The search for the fix becomes a lifelong project.

What is often missed in that search is something simple.

Before there was a pattern, before there was a diagnosis, before there was a story about what is wrong with you, there was something worth protecting.

You protect what matters.

And what matters most inside every human being is remarkably consistent. Your sense of worth. Your wholeness. Your vulnerability—the soft, undefended interior that knows what it needs, feels what it feels, and wants what it wants.

These things do not disappear under pressure. They do not crumble under difficult conditions or complicated relationships. They remain intact. But the system learns very early that they are not always safe to show. And so it does what any intelligent system does when something precious is at risk: it builds protection around it.

Protection is not pathology. It is one of the most fundamental expressions of being human—the instinct to preserve what is vulnerable when conditions make that vulnerability feel risky.

Protection forms around a question the system learns to ask:

Which parts of me are acceptable here?

The answer is never *all of me*. Not in any family, any culture, or any relationship. Some expressions are welcomed easily. Others meet discomfort, distance, or confusion. A system that is paying close attention—which yours was from the very beginning—learns quickly what can come forward and what must remain somewhere else.

Over time, this creates two sides of protection.

On one side are the parts of you that learned to come forward. The capable one. The easy one. The one who did not need too much. These parts became the version of you that moved most easily through the world because they worked. They kept relationships steady. They kept connection intact.

On the other side are the parts that learned to stay back. The ones that felt too much, needed too much, wanted too much. When they surfaced, they seemed to create tension or distance in the people around you. Those parts did not disappear. They moved inward, held behind the same system that was trying, all along, to preserve what was most vulnerable.

Both sides are protection.

Both sides arise from the same instinct: keep what matters out of reach of what might reject it.

I came to understand this through my own experience. For a long time there were parts of me I experienced as problems. One became vigilant and controlling, scanning ahead for what might go wrong. Another moved quickly to manage situations before they became uncomfortable. If a conversation felt tense, I smoothed it over. If a situation felt unstable, I tried to arrange it. I experienced these responses as overreactions, signs that I was anxious or controlling in ways I should not be.

What shifted was not the behavior but my understanding of it. Instead of asking how to eliminate these responses, I began asking what they had been protecting.

I saw how they formed in environments where staying ahead of rupture mattered, where continuity depended on anticipation, and where responsiveness was safer than waiting. These parts were not failures. They were intelligent attempts to preserve connection under the conditions that shaped them.

When I stopped treating them as problems to eliminate, their intensity softened. Not through force, but through recognition. Once the system no longer had to defend its own protection, the protection itself became less rigid, responding more to the present than to the past.

Living inside this architecture has a cost, though it is often difficult to name.

It can be lonely.

Not because you are alone, but because the parts of you that most want to be known are the ones you learned to keep hidden. The parts most visible to others are often the ones that formed to maintain connection. Relationships become possible, but they are rarely complete. You are with people, but not entirely with them.

Something is always held back.

And yet the need for connection never disappears. Being human means reaching toward others. Even within this protective structure, the reaching continues.

But the reaching and the pulling back often happen at the same time.

One part of you longs to be known. It is tired of the distance and wants to be met directly. Another part of you is wary of exactly that, because being known means being seen, and being seen risks exposing the very vulnerability the system learned to protect. You move toward closeness and away from it simultaneously. You invite people in and then hesitate once they are near.

This conflict is often misunderstood.

The person who cannot stop seeking reassurance. The one who withdraws when things become too close. The one who tests the relationship before trusting it. The one who gives everything and then collapses.

These responses are often labeled dysfunction. Yet when understood in context, they reveal something else entirely: a system trying to reach for connection while also protecting what it fears might be rejected.

I once worked with a woman who described herself as avoidant and emotionally shut down. She had heard those descriptions from previous therapists, from her partner, and eventually from herself. But when we began to notice when the shutdown appeared, a pattern emerged. It happened when she was overwhelmed, when too much was being asked of her, when her system had reached its limit.

The shutdown was not a failure of emotional availability. It was protection.

Once she could see it this way, something shifted. Instead of fighting the response, she began to recognize when she was approaching her limit and allowed space before the shutdown arrived. The protection had been doing exactly what it was designed to do.

What changed was not the protection itself. What changed was her relationship to it.

This is where the process of unbecoming begins—not with the elimination of protection, but with the recognition of it.

What was this protecting? What did it cost? What is it still trying to preserve?

Protection does not persist because something went wrong. It persists because it once worked. The nervous system does not abandon what it has preserved simply because circumstances have changed. It loosens only when it no longer has to defend its own necessity.

Which means the way forward is not force. It is recognition. The slow realization that what you have been calling your problem was, for a long time, your solution.

You were not broken. You were protecting something that mattered.

Chapter 5

Change Happens Through Relationship

Most approaches to change begin with the assumption that it happens through private effort and insight gained in solitude. We read, reflect, journal, and analyze. We identify the origin of a pattern and commit to behaving differently. When the pattern returns, when the insight fades, when the response we worked so hard to change appears again, we assume we did not try hard enough and return to the work.

This model is sincere. Yet it misses something fundamental about how human beings change.

Change happens the way it always has: through relationship.

Before we can hold our own experience, someone else holds it for us. A child encounters fear, grief, or overwhelm—states that are real and large, far larger than the child can contain alone. What makes those experiences bearable is not the child's capacity to manage them but the presence of another person who can remain with them. The emotion is shared. The nervous system settles. The experience becomes survivable not because the child handled it, but because they did not have to handle it alone.

This is how capacity develops. Not through effort or exposure, but through being met. Repeated experiences of having distress received and emotions shared gradually build the internal architecture that allows a person to hold their own experience. The relational holding comes first; the internal holding follows.

Something else develops alongside this capacity: the experience of being known.

To allow experience to be held by another is to allow something very interior to be seen—the vulnerable place that earlier principles described as wholeness. When that interior is met with openness rather than judgment, a shift occurs that private effort cannot produce. The isolation of managing alone gives way to the relief of being received. This is the foundation of real connection, both with others and with ourselves.

When change is approached only as a private project, this possibility is often missed. Insight may deepen while experience remains held at a distance. Inner responses are observed, interpreted, or managed rather than met. Understanding accumulates, yet the nervous system does not reorganize, because it does not reorganize through understanding alone. It reorganizes through contact.

Life can continue to function and even appear full while feeling subtly removed. There may be activity without presence, reflection without ease. Something essential remains just out of reach—not because it is missing, but because it has not yet been met.

Relationship, in this context, is not limited to what happens between people. It describes how experience itself is approached. Sensation, emotion, and internal response can either be met in contact or monitored and kept at a distance.

When an inner response is treated as something to override or correct, it remains isolated and protection stays in place. When it is met with attention and allowed to remain without pressure to change, it no longer has to organize itself alone. It gains room to move.

Being seen alters how experience is held. When what is most interior is met with presence rather than judgment—whether within oneself or between people—the body shifts. What was once contained becomes lived. What was managed begins to integrate.

I came to understand this through my relationship with a part of myself that withdrew during moments of emotional intensity. When closeness increased or emotion sharpened, something in me pulled back. For a long time, I treated this as a problem, something to push through or correct. I tried to stay engaged by force.

What changed was not the response but my orientation toward it. Instead of pushing against the withdrawal, I allowed it to be present. I noticed what it needed—slowness, space, less demand—and began to relate to it as a protective response rather than a limitation. In doing so, I was allowing a part of my own nature to be seen by me. That shift mattered more than any attempt to behave differently.

As the internal relationship changed, my relationships with others began to change as well. Staying present required less effort. Vulnerability felt less dangerous. Distance was no longer necessary for stability.

I once worked with a couple where the man had spent years holding a particular part of himself back—a fear he considered weak and a tenderness he had learned to keep covered. During a session, he shared something he had never told anyone. He spoke slowly, watching his wife's face, braced for the reaction he had always expected: disappointment, withdrawal, or the confirmation that this part of him was too much.

His wife did not try to fix it. She did not reassure him or move quickly past the discomfort. She simply stayed present and allowed what he said to land.

When he finished, there was a long moment of quiet. Then something in him released. He let out a breath, looked at her, and said, "It's like I've had this plate over my chest my whole life. And I just took it off. I can show you my squishy inside, and it's okay."

He was describing the experience of his essential nature being seen. The squishy inside was the tender interior he had spent years protecting. The plate was everything that had kept it covered. In that moment—when his vulnerability was simply met—the protection was no longer necessary. Change occurred not because the fear had been fixed, but because his nature had been allowed to be known and received.

When change is understood as relational, attention shifts. The question is no longer how to force a different response, but how experience is being met—what is allowed to remain present and what is still held apart.

The impulse to handle everything privately begins to soften. Being affected by your own experience, or by another person, becomes less threatening. Internal responses that once required distance may remain closer, not because they have been resolved, but because they are no longer alone.

Over time, this changes the quality of presence itself. Less energy is spent maintaining separation, and more becomes available for contact. Life begins to feel less like something to work on and more like something to live.

The parts that were most carefully hidden—the tender, vulnerable interior—turn out to be the very parts that make real contact possible. They do not need to be fixed before they can be known.

They only need to be met.

Chapter 6

The Human Condition Is Complete

Human beings have always searched for a way to understand how to live.

We look for it in religion, philosophy, psychology, and self-help. We listen to teachers. We read books that promise clarity. Somewhere in the search is the hope that life will eventually make sense—that there is a framework or insight that will finally explain how to be here.

Yet the basic structure of being human has never been hidden.

It is visible everywhere.

Every life begins the same way: with birth. A person arrives into a world they did not choose, into a body they did not design, into relationships and conditions that were already unfolding long before they appeared.

From that moment forward, life moves through realities that no one escapes.

We grow. We attach to people. We lose them. We begin things, and we watch them end.

Love appears. Illness arrives. Bodies strengthen and eventually weaken.

Entire civilizations rise and fall within the span of human history. Families form, fracture, and begin again. Children are born into the same world where others are grieving, building, fighting, forgiving, and starting over.

None of this stands outside the human condition.

Yet many of us spend years approaching these realities as though they should not exist. We imagine that life will eventually settle into a stable version of itself—one where the good remains and the difficult parts disappear. We hope for love without loss, beginnings without endings, growth without decline.

When the harder realities arrive—as they always do—they feel like interruptions. Something must have gone wrong.

But the human condition has never promised that kind of stability.

Life moves in cycles that are older than any preference we might have about how it should feel. The natural world reflects this continuously. Seasons turn without asking whether we are ready for them. Growth gives way to decay. Something begins, flourishes for a time, and eventually falls away.

Nothing in these movements is considered a mistake.

A seed disappears into dark soil before it germinates. Trees shed their leaves not because something has failed, but because that is how life continues. What looks like loss is often the beginning of the next cycle.

Human life unfolds in much the same way.

There are seasons of expansion and seasons of contraction. Periods when things come together and periods when they fall apart. Relationships deepen and sometimes end. Bodies grow strong and eventually grow tired. New life appears while other lives quietly conclude.

For a long time, I treated these realities as problems to manage. When things were going well, I tried to preserve them. When life shifted—when uncertainty arrived, or something, ended—I searched for the explanation that might restore the stability I thought I had lost.

It took years to realize that nothing had gone wrong.

Life had simply moved.

I once worked with a man who struggled with endings. He stayed in jobs too long, relationships too long, and even conversations too long. Letting something conclude felt unbearable, as though it meant failure.

One afternoon, he began describing his garden.

He talked about planting in the spring, about the satisfaction of watching the plants fill out during the summer. He described the moment in early fall when the leaves began to yellow, and the tomato vines stopped producing fruit.

"You can't fight it," he said. "It's their time. You thank them for what they gave you and clear the space for what comes next."

He paused mid-sentence.

"Oh," he said quietly.

The understanding was already there in his hands. He had been living it in the soil of his garden. The cycle he accepted without question in the natural world was the same cycle he had been resisting everywhere else.

The human condition is not something we graduate from. It is the landscape we live within.

I saw this even more clearly the first time I sat beside someone who was dying. The room was quiet in a way that felt strangely ordinary. Outside the window, cars were moving through the street. Someone was laughing somewhere down the hallway. Life was continuing at its usual pace.

Inside the room, a life was slowly ending. Nothing in the wider world paused to make space for it. The movement of life and the presence of death existed side by side.

For a long time, that seemed difficult to understand. *How could both be true at once?*

But this is the structure of being human.

Birth happens in the same world where people are dying. Joy appears in the middle of grief. Love grows in the same life that will eventually contain loss.

None of these realities cancel the others. They are simply part of the same landscape.

To be human is to move continuously through these realities: to be born, to grow, to love, to lose, to change, and eventually to die. These experiences are not interruptions to life.

They are what life is made of.

When this becomes clear, the effort spent trying to construct a life without difficulty begins to loosen. The full range of being human—its beauty, its fragility, its uncertainty—starts to appear less like a problem and more like the terrain itself.

The map we have been searching for has never been hidden. It is written into the rhythms of the world, into the cycles of living things, and into the ordinary unfolding of a human life. Nothing essential has been left out.

The difficulty has never been that life is incomplete. The difficulty is that we often try to accept only part of it.

But the human condition does not arrive in pieces. It arrives whole—containing beginnings and endings, love and loss, growth and decline, creation and destruction.

Everything we need to understand how to be here is already present in the life we are living.

The map was never somewhere else.

It has always been the land itself.

Interlude: The First and Last Teachers

Before any philosophy or framework, every human life encounters the same two events.

Birth.

And death.

They stand at opposite ends of the same arc, shaping everything that happens in between.

Birth is the first teacher.

A human life appears without having done anything to earn its place here. A newborn has accomplished nothing, proven nothing, contributed nothing. Yet the moment the child arrives, the entire room reorganizes itself around that fragile presence.

Voices soften. Hands reach out instinctively. Attention gathers.

The smallest movements carry weight—the rise and fall of a tiny chest, the opening of the eyes, the sound of breath filling lungs that have never breathed before.

What people feel in that moment is difficult to name, but it is unmistakable. Even those who struggle to believe that human beings possess inherent worth often sense it when a newborn is placed in their arms.

The life they are holding is completely vulnerable. Entirely dependent. Unable to survive without care.

And yet no one questions whether that life deserves to exist. The worth is obvious. The dignity is assumed.

Something in us recognizes it immediately. The instinct to protect arrives before thought. Adults who were strangers a moment ago begin orienting themselves around the fragile presence in the room. Bodies move closer. Attention sharpens. The environment rearranges itself around the task of keeping this life safe.

The child has done nothing to create this response. The response arises because a human life is here.

Birth reveals something simple and easy to forget: a person begins life already whole. Not perfected, not developed, not accomplished—whole in the most basic sense of being alive and worthy of care.

This is the condition we all arrive in.

A life that will eventually learn, adapt, protect, attach, and change. A life that will grow into relationships, into identity, into the long unfolding of being human.

Which brings us to the second teacher.

Death.

If birth announces the arrival of a life, death reminds us that every life will eventually end.

No person is promised a particular length of time. Some lives stretch across many decades. Others conclude much sooner than anyone expected. Death does not follow a predictable schedule. It does not wait for life to feel complete.

Yet its presence shapes the way life is lived.

When death becomes visible—when someone we love becomes ill, when we stand beside a hospital bed, when we sit quietly at a funeral—something shifts in our attention. The ordinary noise of life grows quieter. Concerns that once felt urgent lose their intensity.

In those moments the question of what matters becomes unexpectedly clear.

Who matters.

What we wish we had said.

What we wish we had done differently.

What we are grateful for.

Death does not create meaning so much as reveal it. The fact that life ends places a frame around everything inside it. Within that frame, values begin to crystallize. Attention gathers around what is real and falls away from what was merely distracting.

Birth and death are events every human life encounters.

One reminds us that we arrived already worthy of care and protection. The other reminds us that the time we have here is finite.

Between those two points unfolds everything else.

Love and loss. Creation and destruction. Beginnings and endings.

People enter our lives and eventually leave them. Bodies grow strong and eventually grow tired. Entire seasons of life appear and fade.

For a long time, many of us search for the right philosophy or system that might explain how to navigate these realities. We look for the framework that will tell us how to live.

But birth and death have been teaching the same lessons all along.

Life begins in vulnerability and dependence. It unfolds through relationship, change, and adaptation. It moves through cycles of growth and decline. And eventually, it ends.

Nothing about this structure is accidental.

It is the human condition.

When we stop resisting the full shape of that condition—when we stop trying to construct a version of life that includes only the parts we prefer—something begins to settle.

The urgency to fix ourselves softens. The effort to control every outcome loosens its grip. What remains is a clearer view of the life that is already here.

A life that began in inherent dignity.

A life that will one day end.

And the long, complex, beautiful stretch of being human that unfolds in between.

What Begins to Shift

When the premise is that we are not enough, healing becomes a job. It becomes an endless, exhausting quest to locate the exact source of our brokenness and apply the correct intervention.

From this ground, we learn to treat our own lives with suspicion. We monitor our reactions, track our progress, and interpret ordinary human experiences—grief, confusion, reactivity, fatigue—as problems to solve. We assume that if we are still struggling, we must be missing something. We search for the next insight, replay the past over and over, and look for the one stone left to turn that will finally be the breakthrough that makes the difference. The effort is sincere, but it is fueled by a deficit. And because the premise is that we are flawed, the work is never finished.

But when the premise changes, the effort changes with it.

When the principles of unbecoming begin to take root—when wholeness is assumed rather than earned—the rest begins to fall into place, often without much effort at all. What follows name that shift. They are not new rules to follow, goals to achieve, or states to maintain. They are descriptions of what naturally happens when you stop organizing your life around the belief that something is wrong with you.

They are the realizations that emerge when the effort to fix being human finally softens.

Chapter 7

Patterns Loosen

A woman I worked with had a habit of over-explaining herself.

Every boundary arrived with a paragraph of justification. Every preference was followed by a careful explanation of why it was reasonable. She knew the pattern well and disliked it intensely. Many times she had tried to stop, only to find the words already leaving her mouth before she had even decided to speak.

Then one day, she said no to something and simply stopped talking.

The silence that followed felt enormous. She could feel the explanation assembling itself in her mind, the familiar speech forming almost automatically. But the urgency behind it had softened. The person in front of her did not require convincing, and the need to persuade dissolved.

The old track was still visible.

She was simply no longer standing on it.

Later, she described the moment not as a victory, but as a surprise.

Experiences like this begin to appear once the principles settle into the background of how life is understood. Life itself does not immediately look different. The same situations arise. The same emotions move through the body. Old reactions still show up with familiar timing.

What changes first is not the pattern.

It is the way the pattern is noticed.

Something subtle becomes visible: the effort. Not the obvious effort of work or responsibility, but the effort that organizes much of inner life—the effort to stabilize what feels uncertain, to improve what feels uncomfortable, to guide experience toward something more manageable.

For a long time, this effort feels natural, even responsible. It resembles care. It resembles maturity. When something feels off, attention moves quickly to interpret it. A sensation appears, and the mind traces it backward, searching for the thought or event that might explain it. An emotion arises and is evaluated—whether it makes sense, whether it should be there, whether something should be done about it.

Over time, this movement becomes so continuous that it fades into the background. It no longer feels like an action. It begins to feel like the normal condition of being alive.

Occasionally, though, something interrupts the rhythm.

I noticed this one afternoon while sitting with a familiar wave of anxiety. The sensation was easy to recognize—the tightening in my chest, the low hum of dread gathering beneath the surface. Ordinarily, that sensation would have triggered the same sequence of responses: analyzing the feeling, tracing it back to something, attempting to regulate it until it subsided.

The impulse was there, but this time it carried no momentum.

It was like a machine turning over without catching. The familiar machinery of figuring and fixing simply remained idle. And in the space where that effort usually lived, there was only the sensation itself.

Without the constant movement of interpretation, the anxiety behaved differently than I expected. It had texture. It had rhythm. It rose and fell the way weather moves through a landscape, shifting without instruction.

The feeling itself was not fixed.

What had been fixed was the response to it.

When the effort isn't there, the experience becomes simply an experience.

This is often what it looks like when a pattern begins to loosen. Not a dramatic breakthrough or a triumph of will, but an absence. Something that once organized behavior simply loses its authority.

Patterns rarely loosen because we confront them more forcefully. They loosen because the conditions that once required them begin to change. When the assumption that something must constantly be corrected softens, the effort organized around that assumption softens as well.

And when effort loosens, experience has room to move.

What once felt permanent begins to look more like a path through soft earth—one that fades gradually when it is no longer walked each day.

Pause and Notice

Think of a familiar pattern.

Right before it begins, what effort appears alongside it?

What happens when that effort is allowed to soften, even briefly?

When the pattern does not run, what remains?

Chapter 8

Integration Matter More Than Insight

I once sat in my car after a difficult conversation, replaying the exchange in my mind the way people often do when something doesn't land quite right. By the time I turned the key in the ignition, I understood exactly what had happened. I could see the childhood pattern clearly, the protective strategy that had shaped the moment, the old fear underneath it that had guided the response. The logic of it all was obvious once I looked closely enough. I could have explained the whole thing to someone else in a few sentences.

The insight was complete. And the next time a similar conversation happened, the same response appeared, as automatic as breathing.

For a long time, this puzzled me. Understanding had changed the story I told about the moment, but it had not touched the body living it. The reaction still arrived with the same timing, the same familiar pull. The explanation had grown clearer, yet the pattern itself remained.

Experiences like this begin to stand out once the principles settle into the background of how life is understood. Understanding often comes more easily. Patterns become easier to recognize. Connections form between past and present, between a reaction and the conditions that once shaped it. Experiences that once felt confusing begin to organize themselves into something coherent, and for a while, that clarity can feel like progress.

Insight carries an unspoken promise. If something finally makes sense—if a pattern can be traced back to its origin and understood clearly enough—it seems reasonable to expect that the pattern will begin to loosen. Understanding suggests movement. It feels like the kind of progress that should matter.

For a long time, I believed that this clarity was the work.

Over time, though, it becomes harder to ignore the difference between insight and change. Understanding can describe what is happening with remarkable precision, yet the system that carries the response often continues as it always has. The explanation becomes more accurate, but the reaction remains familiar.

Experience does not reorganize itself through explanation alone. The body changes through what is lived.

These moments rarely arrive as breakthroughs. More often, they appear in the middle of ordinary life: a moment when you brace for criticism, and the person in front of you simply stays present; a moment when you speak honestly, expecting distance, and the relationship does not collapse; a moment when you rest, certain that everything will unravel, and nothing does.

The mind may register these moments quickly and move on, but the body keeps a different kind of record. It notices what actually happens rather than what has been understood. Over time, these small experiences accumulate, gradually reshaping what the system expects from the world.

I saw this clearly with someone I worked with who believed her worth depended on her productivity. She knew the belief well. She had traced it back to its origins, talked about it in therapy, and read the books that explained it. She could describe exactly how the pattern had formed and why it continued to shape her life. But she still could not rest without guilt.

Then she got sick. Nothing serious, just enough to keep her home for a week. She had no choice but to stop working. The days passed slowly. She slept, read, and watched the light move through the room as the hours unfolded.

And her life continued. People still cared about her. Her responsibilities were still there when she returned. The world had not collapsed because she stopped producing for a few days.

Her body learned something her mind had already known.

After that week, rest felt different—not because she had gained a new insight, but because the system that carried the belief had experienced something that contradicted it.

Integration often moves this way. Not through understanding alone, but through lived moments that alter what the body expects from the world. Insight does not disappear, but its role begins to change. It becomes a way of describing what experience has already begun to reorganize, rather than a tool for forcing that reorganization.

This is why change can feel strangely uneventful even when it is real. Life on the outside may look very much the same. Inside, something is no longer working as hard to hold itself together.

The difference is lived.

Pause and Notice

Think of something you understand clearly about yourself, but do not fully feel in your body.

What kind of lived experience might gently contradict the belief underneath it?

Not a breakthrough. Just a small moment where something happens differently than expected.

Where in your life might that already be unfolding?

Chapter 9

Wholeness Includes Contradiction

I remember sitting with a close friend one evening and noticing something that once would have confused me. I felt deeply connected to her—the warmth, the familiarity, the ease that comes from years of knowing someone well. And at the same time, something in me felt slightly distant, as though a part of me was holding back.

For a long time, I would have tried to determine which feeling was the real one. Was I close to this person or not? The contradiction would have felt unstable, as though it required an answer before the moment could settle.

But both experiences were simply there.

Neither cancelled the other out.

Recognition like this begins to appear once the principles settle into the background of how life is understood. Many people expect that inner life will become clearer or more coherent, that emotions will organize themselves into something stable once the work of understanding begins. The assumption is that growth will eventually produce a kind of internal harmony in which responses align and contradiction fades.

What becomes visible instead is complexity.

Different experiences begin to register simultaneously. Relief may exist alongside grief. Openness may appear with hesitation. A desire to move forward can live beside an equally real desire to stay where things are familiar. These responses do not cancel one another out. They arise together, each shaped by its own conditions.

For most of us, this complexity is difficult to tolerate at first.

There is a kind of internal accounting that runs beneath experience. Certain states are marked as good—calm, clear, connected, motivated. Others are marked as evidence that something has gone wrong—anxious, sad, reactive, flat. The accounting happens quickly, often before the feeling itself is fully recognized. A state appears, meaning is assigned to it, and the mind begins organizing around what should be done.

Over time, this evaluative lens begins to feel like common sense.

For much of my life, I trusted the states that felt good and questioned the ones that didn't. When I felt grounded, I took it as confirmation that something was going right. When anxiety returned, or sadness, or the particular flatness that sometimes settles in without explanation, I assumed something had slipped out of place, and attention moved quickly toward repair.

What I did not see for a long time was that the accounting itself was shaping the experience. Not the anxiety or the sadness, but the meaning I assigned to their arrival. Beneath the evaluation was an assumption that wholeness should feel a certain way—that if something uncomfortable appeared, it must signal a problem that required attention.

Over time, it became harder to maintain that assumption. Life continued to fluctuate, just as it always has. There were periods of ease and periods of difficulty, stretches of clarity and stretches of fog, days when everything felt inhabitable and days when nothing did. Gradually, the movement itself began to look less like a problem and more like the ordinary rhythm of being alive.

The human condition moves this way.

I worked with someone who described a similar tension in her relationship to her work. She loved it—the meaning, the connection with the people she served, the sense that what she did mattered. And she resented it—the demands, the emotional weight, the way it followed her home at the end of the day.

She kept trying to determine which feeling was true. If she loved the work, the resentment shouldn't be there. If the resentment was real, perhaps she had chosen the wrong path. The contradiction felt unstable, as though it required a decision before she could rest.

Eventually, something shifted.

She stopped trying to extract a single conclusion from the tension. The love remained. The resentment remained. The work was meaningful and exhausting at the same time.

When the demand for coherence softened, the pressure eased. The contradiction did not disappear. It simply stopped being treated as a problem.

This is often what wholeness looks like from the inside. Not a single clean emotion, but multiple experiences existing at the same time without needing to cancel one another out. Grief and peace after someone dies. Love and frustration within the same relationship. The desire for change alongside the wish to stay exactly where you are.

The evaluative lens struggles with these moments because it assumes only one thing can be true at a time. It looks for a verdict.

But human experience rarely arrives that way.

We are large enough to contain more than one truth.

Wholeness does not require internal coherence. It holds what appears inconsistent without asking it to reconcile. When experience is no longer divided into what is acceptable and what must be corrected, something begins to relax—not necessarily into ease, but into honesty.

The fluctuation remains. The contradiction remains.

What disappears is the demand that experience resolve itself before it is allowed to belong.

Pause and Notice

Where do opposing feelings or impulses appear together in your experience right now?

What usually happens when that tension appears—does the mind move toward resolution, explanation, or avoidance?

What shifts when both experiences are allowed to remain without deciding which one is correct?

Chapter 10

Time is Not Linear

For years, the sound of heavy footsteps on the floor above me would send a jolt of adrenaline through my body.

My upstairs neighbor was a gentle, quiet person. There was no threat. But the sound of those footsteps—firm, sudden, unmistakable—would tighten something inside me before I had time to think. My heart would start pounding. My breath would shorten. For a moment, I would freeze, completely still, as if waiting for something that had not yet happened.

Nothing ever did.

The footsteps would continue across the ceiling, the refrigerator would hum softly in the kitchen, and the ordinary quiet of the apartment would return. Intellectually, I knew where I was. I knew I was safe. But my body had already traveled somewhere else.

It had gone back to a different house, a different set of footsteps, a time when that sound meant something very different.

Experiences like this become easier to recognize once the principles begin to settle into the background of how life is understood. At first, they can feel confusing. A reaction appears that seems disproportionate to the moment. The body tightens. Attention sharpens. Urgency moves in quickly, even when the circumstances themselves do not require it.

When growth is imagined as moving forward, these moments can feel discouraging. There is often an assumption that once something has been understood or worked through, it should remain behind us. When an old response returns, it can appear as though nothing has changed.

What gradually becomes clearer is that experience does not organize itself chronologically.

While the mind separates past from present, the body responds to familiarity. It registers tone, posture, proximity, and the subtle signals of relationship long before conscious thought has time to interpret them. A moment that resembles an earlier one can elicit the same response, even when the present situation is entirely different.

The past does not remain contained as memory alone. It continues to shape how the present is met—not as something recalled deliberately, but as something anticipated. A tone of voice, a particular kind of silence, the feeling of being watched or ignored can be enough to bring an old response fully online.

In those moments, it can feel as though two times are happening at once.

I noticed this most clearly when defensiveness would arise in situations that did not call for it. A simple question could tighten my chest or stir the impulse to explain myself quickly, even in relationships where curiosity and care were present. The response did not reflect what was happening so much as what had once been necessary.

At first, the return of those reactions felt disorienting, as though it contradicted what I knew about my current life. Over time, the meaning of the return began to shift. Instead of reading it as failure, it became information about what my system had learned earlier and had not yet fully updated through experience.

I worked with someone who described a similar moment with her partner during dinner one evening. He asked a simple question about her day—an ordinary, curious question—but something in the tone sent her immediately into defense. Her jaw tightened. Her mind began assembling an explanation before she even understood why.

Later, she realized that the response belonged to a different time. She had grown up in a home where questions meant an attack. Curiosity often carried accusation. Every answer was examined for evidence of failure or dishonesty.

Her partner's question was not an interrogation, but her body did not know that yet.

Change began when she could notice the response without immediately acting on it. She could feel the surge of defensiveness and, at the same time, see her partner's open, attentive face. She could feel the past and still remain in contact with the present.

The response did not disappear immediately. But it began to have less authority.

This is often what the lived truth of non-linear time looks like. The work is not to erase the past or prevent old responses from appearing. It is to remain present enough that the system can gradually register that the conditions have changed.

I eventually noticed this with the footsteps above my apartment as well. The sound would arrive, the jolt of adrenaline would follow, and for a moment, the past would press itself against the present. But alongside the pounding heart I could also feel the solid floor beneath my feet, hear the refrigerator humming, see the light moving across the room.

The response was still there.

But it was no longer the only thing there.

Time felt less like a line I was trying to move beyond and more like a space I was living within. The past was still in that space, the future was there too, but my life was happening here, now, in the present that continued unfolding around me.

Pause and Notice

Where do familiar responses appear even when your present circumstances feel different from the past?

What does it feel like in your body when a moment from the past seems to return inside the present?

What small detail in your environment right now reminds you that you are here—in this room, in this moment, in the life you are living today?

Chapter 11

Wholeness is Shared

I once sat in a circle of people as someone spoke about a shame he had carried for most of his life. It was the kind of shame that usually remains hidden—the unspoken belief that something about you is fundamentally wrong, that if others truly saw this part of you, they would step back, or turn away, or confirm the fear you already carry.

He spoke slowly, carefully, as though each sentence had to cross a threshold before it could be said aloud. As he continued, something in the room shifted. People leaned forward slightly. The atmosphere softened. A kind of collective stillness settled over the group.

What was most striking was not only his courage in speaking, but also the expressions on everyone's faces. Again and again, I saw the same reaction: recognition. It wasn't exactly sympathy, and it wasn't exactly surprise. It was the visceral understanding that comes when someone names something you have felt yourself.

You could see it in the softened eyes, the small nods, the subtle exhale that moved through the room as he spoke. The feeling he was describing—so private to him, so heavy with secrecy—was not unfamiliar to the people hearing it.

They knew that feeling.

In that moment, his shame was no longer only his. It had become part of something shared. The shame itself did not disappear, but its weight changed. The isolation that had held it in place softened, not because anyone tried to fix it, but because it was no longer being carried alone.

Experiences like this become easier to recognize once the principles settle into the background of how life is understood.

For most of us, there is a kind of loneliness that has nothing to do with being physically alone. It is the loneliness of believing that our experience is uniquely ours—that the fears we carry, the doubts we wrestle with, the ache of not being enough somehow belong only to us.

We are often taught, implicitly and explicitly, to interpret these experiences as personal failings. Evidence that something about us is deficient or incomplete. What we are rarely taught is that these feelings are not signs of our inadequacy but expressions of the human condition itself. The feeling of not being enough, the fear of being too much, the suspicion that no one really sees you—these are not rare experiences. They are woven into the texture of being human.

The specifics of your story are uniquely yours, but the essence of what you feel is shared across countless lives, in countless rooms, across generations that lived long before you did.

Recognizing this begins to shift the relationship to experience in subtle ways. What once felt like a private defect begins to look more like participation in something larger than the self.

I began to notice this most clearly in relationships. For much of my life, I experienced regulation as a personal responsibility. If something felt tense in a conversation, I assumed I had failed to manage myself properly. If distance appeared in a relationship, I believed it was my job to correct it.

Over time, that understanding began to loosen. I started noticing how much of what we experience happens between people rather than within them. Breath slows when someone nearby settles. Attention sharpens when someone listens closely. Tension softens when it is met rather than resisted.

The nervous system does not operate in isolation. It responds constantly to what happens around it—to tone, presence, proximity, and the subtle signals of relationship.

Someone once described sitting beside a friend during a difficult moment in her life. She wasn't looking for advice or solutions; she was only looking for someone willing to sit with her. Her friend did not try to fix anything or offer reassurance. She simply stayed close, occasionally placing a hand on her arm, breathing slowly beside her.

After a few minutes, she noticed something unexpected. Her own breath had begun to match her friend's rhythm without her deciding to change it. The tightness in her chest softened slightly. The urgency that had been driving her thoughts slowed.

Nothing had been solved. The difficulty she was facing remained exactly where it was. But something in her system shifted because she was no longer carrying it alone.

Connection often works this way.

There is another way life is shared as well. Someone I worked with once told me that she and her partner had spent years trying to "work on" their relationship. They read books on communication, practiced conflict-resolution techniques, and spent long evenings analyzing disagreements. The relationship slowly became a project that always required improvement.

Eventually, they started a small garden together.

At first, it had nothing to do with their relationship. They were simply planting vegetables, pulling weeds, watering the soil, watching what grew and what did not. But something changed in the middle of that ordinary activity. They were no longer working on the relationship. They were simply doing something together—standing in the dirt, passing tools back and forth, watching the slow progress of the seasons.

In those quiet moments, they found a different kind of connection, one that did not depend on analysis or repair but on participation in something shared.

Life is shared in both senses.

It is shared internally, in the sense that the struggles we carry are not uniquely ours. And it is shared externally, in the sense that life unfolds between people—in meals prepared together, walks taken side by side, conversations that drift late into the evening, and the countless small activities that make up a life.

Wholeness does not emerge in isolation. It becomes visible in recognizing that our lives are already intertwined with those around us, that what we feel and carry is not separate from the wider human story.

The details belong to you.

But the life moving through them is shared.

Pause and Notice

Where do you feel most alone in your experience?

What story do you tell yourself about that feeling?

What shifts when you imagine that experience not as a personal failing, but as part of a shared human condition?

Where in your life do you notice the ease of shared activity—moments where connection arises simply from doing something alongside another person?

Chapter 12

Reorientation, Not Resolution

A woman I once worked with told me about something she began noticing in the middle of ordinary moments. She would find herself deep inside a familiar story—convinced she had said the wrong thing, certain that someone was upset with her, replaying a conversation again and again in her mind. For a while, the story would feel completely convincing. Her body would tighten, her thoughts would accelerate, and the old narrative would gather momentum, as it always had.

Then, at some point, something small would interrupt it. Sometimes it was a breath. Sometimes it was a pause between thoughts. Sometimes it was simply the realization that she had been here before. In that moment, she would think, almost with surprise, *Oh. I know this place.* Nothing dramatic happened after that. The feeling didn't vanish. The situation didn't resolve itself. But something subtle shifted in how she was inside it. The story loosened just enough for her to recognize it as a pattern she had traveled through many times before.

She described the experience as remembering—not remembering a fact or a detail, but remembering herself.

For a long time, she had assumed that if she truly understood her patterns, they would stop appearing. Insight, she believed, would bring resolution. The old responses would disappear, replaced by something steadier and more reliable. What surprised her was that the patterns did not vanish. They still arrived with familiar timing. The same reactions appeared in similar moments. The same emotional currents moved through her body.

What changed was how quickly she noticed them. The gap between drifting and remembering began to shorten.

At first, she would spend hours caught inside the old story before realizing what had happened. Later, it was minutes. Then, only a few sentences into the familiar narrative before something in her paused. Eventually, the signal became more subtle—sometimes only a feeling in her chest, a small recognition that she had stepped away from the ground she knew how to stand on.

She began to describe the return not as a correction, but as a kind of homecoming.

For many of us, growth is imagined as movement toward resolution. We expect that understanding should eventually stabilize experience, that emotional work should bring us to a point where the old responses stop appearing altogether. But human life rarely organizes itself that way. Situations remain unfinished. Relationships evolve and reopen. Familiar reactions surface again in new circumstances. The nervous system contracts under pressure, the mind gathers old explanations, and for a while, we are fully inside the story again.

The question is not whether this will happen. The question is what it feels like to return.

Instead of forcing experience toward a final conclusion, attention gradually learns how to reorient itself. The drift still occurs, but it no longer carries the same meaning. It becomes part of the rhythm of being human rather than evidence that something has gone wrong.

I noticed this in my own life when certain patterns kept appearing long after I believed I understood them. There were moments when the old self-criticism returned with surprising intensity, when the mind assembled its familiar case against me with the same persuasive logic it had always used. For a long time, I interpreted those moments as proof that I had missed something—that I had not gone deep enough, or worked hard enough, or fully integrated the insight I thought I had gained.

Eventually, the pattern began to look different. The drifting itself was not the problem. It was simply the nervous system doing what nervous systems do: tightening under pressure, reaching for familiar ways of organizing experience. What mattered was the return.

Sometimes that return felt like relief, a settling back into something steady. Sometimes it carried a trace of grief—a recognition of how long I had been running on the old story before noticing it. Occasionally, it felt almost imperceptible, like a door gently settling back into its frame. But every time it carried the same quality of recognition: this is the ground.

Another client described something similar after the end of a relationship she spent months trying to understand. She replayed conversations, analyzed turning points, and tried to construct a narrative that would explain exactly what had happened. Each time she believed she had found the answer, something complicated the story. A memory of tenderness would surface beside a memory of disconnection. Moments that felt meaningful existed alongside moments that had depleted her.

Eventually, she stopped trying to resolve the question. The relationship had been many things at once—loving and painful, nourishing and limiting. It did not need to collapse into a single conclusion. When she stopped trying to finalize its meaning, something softened. The relationship remained unfinished in a certain way, but it no longer organized her attention.

What had changed was not the past itself, but her orientation to it.

Over time, this becomes the rhythm of living these truths. Attention narrows, drifts, and returns. Old patterns appear and soften. Meaning forms and dissolves as life continues to unfold. The ground itself does not disappear during these movements. It simply waits to be remembered.

The remembering is not the end of the process.

It is the process—playing out in real time, inside an ordinary human life.

Pause and Notice

Where do you find yourself drifting into familiar stories or patterns right now?

When those moments happen, how long does it usually take before you notice?

What does it feel like in your body when you recognize that you have returned—not fixing the moment or resolving it, but simply remembering where you are again?

Already Moving

I have a tendency to move fast in my life sometimes, especially when I'm excited about something. I can get tunnel visioned. I stop noticing what's around me. I'm pulled in. And even if it's positive, I'm just not as *here*.

The return usually starts with an "oh, I did the thing again." The thing is getting lost. It's not paying attention. It's forgetting that I'm a human living a life that is precious and fleeting.

"Oh. Here I am."

The recognition reorients.

It happened recently during a week that was full of good things—projects moving forward, conversations that felt alive, a schedule packed with momentum. I was moving through my days efficiently, checking things off, managing the flow of information and people. I felt capable. I felt useful.

But by Thursday afternoon, I realized I hadn't actually tasted my food in three days. I hadn't felt the temperature of the air when I walked outside. I was having conversations, but I was already three steps ahead of the person speaking, formulating my response before they had finished their sentence. I was managing my life beautifully, but I wasn't actually inside it.

The recognition didn't come as a grand epiphany. It came as a sudden, quiet friction. I was standing in the kitchen, pouring a glass of water, and I felt a familiar tightness in my chest—the physical signature of moving too fast.

Oh. I did the thing again.

In the past, that recognition would have immediately triggered a management strategy. I would have told myself to take three deep breaths. I would have diagnosed my lack of presence as a failure of discipline. I would have tried to force myself back into the moment, turning "being present" into just another task on the list.

This time, I didn't do any of that. I just stood there with the glass of water and let the friction be there.

I let myself feel how tightly wound I was. I let myself feel the momentum that was still trying to pull me forward into the next hour. And as I stayed with it, the structure of that momentum began to loosen. The urgency that had felt so necessary ten minutes earlier started to feel slightly absurd. The identity of the "efficient, capable person getting things done" began to feel like a heavy coat I had forgotten to take off indoors.

I didn't try to take the coat off. I just noticed I was wearing it. And in that noticing, the fabric started to give.

What happened next was not a decision. It was an emergence. I looked at my phone, saw an email I had been planning to answer immediately, and felt a clear, quiet no. Not a rebellious no, not a strategic no. Just the biological reality that my capacity for the day was spent. I set the phone down. I didn't rehearse an apology in my head. I didn't negotiate with myself about when I would answer it later. I just let the boundary exist.

The rest of the evening moved differently. The speed was gone. I sat on the couch and actually felt the weight of my body sinking into the cushions. I listened to my husband talk about his day, and for the first time all week, I wasn't waiting for my turn to speak. I was just listening. The animating force of the evening wasn't my agenda; it was just life, unfolding at its own pace, moving through the room without my supervision.

It felt ordinary. It felt like breathing.

And then, of course, Friday morning arrived. An unexpected conflict surfaced. A deadline shifted. And within twenty minutes, I was back in the tunnel. The jaw tightened. The speed returned. The need to manage and secure and fix took over the dashboard.

I lost it, the old voice whispered. You were doing so well last night, and now you're back at the beginning.

But I wasn't at the beginning. I was just contracted. The nervous system was doing exactly what it was designed to do under pressure—narrowing its focus to handle a perceived threat. The difference was that this time, I didn't believe the contraction was the whole truth. I knew it was just a season of the nervous system. I knew the ground was still there, even if I couldn't feel it in that exact moment.

I didn't fight the speed. I just let it run its course, knowing that eventually, the momentum would break, the recognition would return, and I would find myself standing somewhere quiet again, thinking:

Oh. Here I am.

This is how it moves. Not as a straight line toward a perfected, permanently present self, but as a continuous, breathing rhythm. We get lost. We wake up. We let the armor soften. We feel the life underneath it. We contract again. And we learn to stay with ourselves through all of it.

These are the phases of unbecoming.

The Phases

T he phases are not something new. They are something you have already been living.

Every human being moves through periods of awareness — moments when the gap between who you have been and who you actually are becomes visible. Periods of unraveling, when what you thought was solid loosens. Periods of emerging, when something that was obscured starts to come forward. Periods of aliveness, when life feels inhabited rather than managed. And periods of returning, when you find yourself back somewhere familiar, and the question is not how to escape it but how to be in it.

These movements are not stages of a process you are undertaking. They are the structure of human experience itself. They have been happening your whole life — in the seasons of a relationship, in the arc of a difficult year, in the way a single conversation can shift something that had been fixed for a long time. The phases give language to what was already occurring. They make visible what has always been moving.

What changes when you have language for them is not the experience itself. What changes is the relationship to it. When you recognize that what you are inside has a shape — that it has moved before and will move again — it becomes something you can be in rather than something you have to escape. The phases do not tell you where to go. They tell you where you already are.

They will cycle. They will overlap. You will find yourself in more than one at a time, and you will return to phases you thought you had left behind. This is not failure. This is the rhythm of a life that is actually being lived.

Chapter 13

The Phase of Awareness

The first sign that something is changing is not a decision. It is a moment of recognition, often quiet and arising from within.

It is the moment you are driving and realize your shoulders have been up by your ears for the last ten miles. You do not know why, and you do not try to fix it. You just notice, and in the noticing, they drop a little on their own.

It is hearing yourself give the same explanation you always give and, for the first time, hearing it as a recording. The words come out, but a part of you is watching them, separate from them, with a sense of curiosity.

It is feeling a familiar tightness in your chest during a conversation, and, instead of ignoring it or pushing through it, a question arises on its own: *What is this?* There is no answer. There is just the question, and the space it creates.

These moments are not something to practice or achieve. They are the first signal that the story you have been living in is becoming visible. For a long time, you were inside the story. Now, a part of you is watching it. This phase is about what happens in that gap.

How Adaptation Works

Adaptation was always about survival. For most of human history, that meant the physical world—food, shelter, safety from threat. The nervous system was built for this. It learned quickly, held what it learned, and organized behavior around what kept the body alive.

For most of us now, the physical conditions of survival are largely secured. Unless our home environments were extreme or abusive—or unless we are still living inside circumstances where physical safety is not guaranteed—we are not primarily adapting to physical threat.

But the nervous system did not stop adapting. It turned toward the emotional landscape: belonging, being seen, and the conditions that make connection possible. These are survival needs, too. The adaptations that form around them are just as real, just as intelligent, and just as automatic as anything that develops in response to physical danger.

I worked with a man in his forties who had spent most of his adult life in a state of low-level vigilance. When he entered a room, his attention moved quickly across it, scanning faces, tracking tone, and monitoring shifts in mood. He calibrated himself constantly, adjusting his behavior to match what he sensed was expected.

For years, he assumed this was simply who he was—anxious, hyperaware, a little exhausting to be around even to himself.

Over time, it became clear that this vigilance had been his adaptation. He had grown up in a household where the emotional atmosphere could change without warning, and learning to read it had been essential. His nervous system had done exactly what it was built to do: it adapted to the conditions of his first world and continued operating from that pattern long after those conditions were gone.

When he began to understand it that way—not as a flaw but as intelligence—something in him loosened. Not the vigilance itself, not yet, but the story he had been telling about it.

Conditioning is the shape adaptation takes. It is how the nervous system organizes experience based on what has happened before.

This learning unfolds through repetition, relationship, emotional experience, and culture, often all at once. Through repetition, beliefs gather momentum. What appears to confirm a belief is often the belief itself shaping perception and response in ways that reinforce it.

In relationship, we learn what is welcome and what is not—what leads to connection and what leads to distance. Emotionally intense experiences leave deeper imprints, particularly when they occur before there is enough perspective to understand them.

The cultural environment we are born into also offers a set of ready-made meanings about worth, success, and belonging that we absorb long before we can question them.

Much of what shapes experience does not appear as belief at all. It shows up instead as expectation, hesitation, certainty, or self-explanation—patterns operating largely outside conscious awareness. These patterns reflect how meaning has already taken shape. Experience is not only registered and responded to; it is shaped so the world becomes more navigable.

Much of this shaping occurs before the capacity for reflection is fully available. A child's nervous system is organized around dependency. It has to be. The task of early life is to adapt to the world that exists and to maintain connection with the people on whom survival depends.

The ability to step back and ask whether something is true comes later. By then, the adaptation is already structural, and the meaning is already embedded.

There is a particular quality to the meanings formed in early life that makes them feel total and personal, almost indistinguishable from truth. A young child cannot yet take the perspective of others. The world is organized around the self as its center—not out of selfishness but out of developmental necessity.

When something goes wrong—when connection breaks, when a need goes unmet, when an experience overwhelms—the only available explanation is the self. The conclusions that form in these moments are simple and powerful: something is wrong with me; I caused this; I am too much; I am not enough.

These conclusions are not distortions. They are the most coherent interpretations a developing mind could make with the tools it had.

When experience could be shared—when someone was present, responsive, able to help make sense of what was happening—the meanings that formed remained flexible and could be revised later.

When experience had to be interpreted alone, the system constructed an explanation from what was available. Those meanings persist with such force because they were never revisited from a wider vantage point. They became the vantage point through which later life was interpreted.

The Shape of Your Adaptation

Human beings are meaning-making creatures. From the beginning of life, the nervous system continually interprets what it encounters. This is not primarily an intellectual process. It is bodily and immediate, the system repeatedly asking a single question: what does this mean?

The answers accumulate. Over time, they form the lens through which experience is interpreted. They shape perception, reaction, and expectation.

We rarely notice this lens because it is the medium through which everything else is seen. We do not encounter the world directly; we encounter it through the meanings we have already made of it.

This is not a malfunction. It is evidence of the human system working exactly as it was designed. We learn the rules of our family, our culture, our time and place, and we shape ourselves in ways that allow us to survive within them. It is an elegant survival strategy.

Yet the shape we take in order to survive can eventually narrow the life we are able to live. The meanings that once helped us navigate our early environments can persist long after those environments have changed.

The structure remains even when the world it was built for no longer exists.

How We Make Meaning

None of this could have been avoided. Every human life is shaped by the conditions into which it is born.

No one moves through life untouched. Experience leaves marks. This is not a problem to solve but a condition of being human.

The nervous system that learned to read a room, interpret emotional signals, and construct meaning from limited information is not malfunctioning. It is doing exactly what a human nervous system does.

What follows is not a catalogue of what went wrong. It is a map of how the system works.

Family Systems: Your First World

Your family was your first world. It was where the rules of reality were first learned—not through instruction but through immersion.

You learned who was safe and who was not. You learned which feelings were welcome and which had to be hidden. You learned what brought connection and what brought distance.

This learning was not intellectual. It was bodily. Your survival depended on the people around you, and your nervous system oriented itself toward maintaining that connection.

You learned the subtle shift in a parent's tone, the meaning of a sigh, and the atmosphere that preceded tension. You became skilled at reading the emotional weather of your home because your life required it.

In some families, the weather is stormy. The dysfunction is overt—addiction, chaos, neglect, abuse. The meanings formed in those environments can be stark: the world is not safe; I am on my own.

In many more families, the weather appears calm. From the outside, there may be stability, achievement, even politeness. Yet the emotional air can be thin. Needs may be inconvenient. Sensitivity may be treated as a problem. Love may appear conditional on performance or compliance.

The meanings formed in these environments are often harder to name but no less powerful: something about me must be wrong; I am too much; I am not enough.

Seeing this clearly is not about blame. Parents are them-selves shaped by the worlds that formed them. It is about recognizing the specific curriculum of one's child-hood—the conditions that shaped adaptation and the meanings that made belonging possible.

Those adaptations are evidence of resourcefulness.

Pause and Notice: Family Influence

As you read this, memories or familiar dynamics may have surfaced. There is no need to organize them or draw conclusions. Simply notice what appears—what feels charged, what feels familiar, and what the mind moves past quickly.

Emotionally Difficult Experiences

Many experiences that shape belief do not arrive as ob-vious turning points. They occur while the sense of self is still forming, before language or perspective is available to interpret what is happening.

At that stage of development, experience and identity are intertwined. What cannot yet be understood is inter-preted, and what cannot be contextualized is absorbed into the developing sense of self.

For this reason, emotionally difficult experiences can shape meaning even when they would not be considered traumatic in a conventional sense. Their impact depends less on severity than on the child's capacity to under-stand them at the time.

Some experiences are openly painful. Others occur in environments that are inconsistent, distracted, or unable to meet what is needed.

A child who repeatedly loses connection may conclude that something about them causes it. A child whose feelings receive little acknowledgment may stop expressing them.

These are not errors in perception. They are the most workable interpretations available at the time.

Many shaping experiences are cumulative rather than singular. Repeated criticism, subtle comparison, or a steady sense of not quite fitting can gradually narrow perception. No single event stands out, yet together they teach the system what to expect.

In this way, the past does not remain neatly in the past. What was learned earlier continues organizing experience in the present.

Pause and Notice: Emotionally Difficult Experience

As you read this section, memories or reactions may have surfaced on their own. If something stood out, simply notice its presence.

Cultural Context: The Water We Swim In

No family exists in isolation. Every family lives within the water of a larger culture. We absorb cultural ideas about what it means to be a person—what success looks like, what is beautiful, what is valuable, what counts as good—not as conscious choices but as the air we breathe.

Many contemporary cultures place high value on productivity, independence, self-optimization, and performance. Bodies become projects to improve. Emotions become problems to manage.

Because human beings adapt, we learn these rules as well. We learn to perform competence, to present acceptable versions of ourselves, and to hide what may be judged as weakness.

Over time, the script disappears into the background. It stops feeling like a script and begins to feel like reality.

Pause and Notice: *Cultural Influence*

As you read this, certain cultural ideas may feel immediately familiar. Notice which expectations feel automatic and where you find yourself tightening or correcting yourself in response to them.

The Loop: How Meaning Becomes Reality

Once formed, a belief rarely sits passively in the mind. It organizes perception, influences behavior, and helps shape the situations we enter and create.

Someone who carries the assumption that they are not wanted may enter a room already scanning for signs of rejection. Neutral expressions appear unfriendly. Hesitation replaces initiative. Others respond to that distance by keeping their own.

The resulting experience confirms the original belief.

In this way, the past continues to act in the present. What was learned under earlier conditions continues to shape interpretation, reaction, and behavior long after those conditions are gone.

Pause and Notice: *The Loop*

As you move through daily life, moments may appear that land differently than expected. Notice the response that follows and how it shapes the next moment.

Belief as Learned Orientation

What are often called limiting beliefs rarely appear as explicit thoughts. They function more like orientations to life.

They show up in patterns—how close someone allows themselves to get to others, what risks feel possible, where attention tightens, and how quickly self-correction appears.

I once worked with a woman who described herself as someone who did not take up space. She did not say this critically. It sounded like a neutral fact, as though she were describing a physical trait.

In groups, she spoke softly. She deferred to others' preferences. When she entered a room, her shoulders angled slightly forward, and her body contracted inward.

Over time, the belief beneath the behavior became visible: her presence felt like an imposition. She had learned that occupying space required justification—usefulness, agreeableness, restraint.

In the household where she grew up, her needs had often been treated as excessive. Her body adapted. It learned to take up less space so that she could stay close. The belief was not a thought. It was a posture.

Beliefs narrow awareness because they were shaped under conditions where options were limited. They once supported adaptation. Over time, they begin to constrain experience, patterning life around expectations that no longer reflect present conditions.

Why Insight Alone Is Not Enough

Because these patterns operate beneath conscious awareness, intellectual understanding rarely alters them on its own.

Someone may know they are worthy of love and still feel unwanted in moments of vulnerability. The body organizes experience faster than thought.

The task is not to argue with the belief or replace it with a better idea. The task is to recognize the pattern itself—the tightening in the body, the familiar drop in the stomach, the interpretation that appears before reflection can intervene.

When the pattern becomes visible, the loop that sustains it can also be seen.

Awareness has always been present within that loop—in every performance of the script, in every moment the body braced before the reason was understood.

What shaped that awareness—the meanings formed in early life, the rules absorbed from family and culture—became the lens through which experience is interpreted. And a lens, by its nature, is the last thing we see through.

The Phase of Awareness begins when that lens itself comes into view. Not to dismantle it. Not to correct what it produced. Only to recognize the shape it has given awareness and begin relating to it directly rather than living entirely within it.

The Nature of Orientation

All of that—the meaning made in your first world, the family rules absorbed before you could question them, the cultural script, the loop—is what awareness has been organized around. What goes unexamined is not awareness itself, but how attention has learned to orient. Awareness does not move, narrow, expand, arrive, or disappear. What changes is attention—where it goes, what it tracks, and how it shapes itself in response to the world.

Very early in life, attention learned to move outward. Long before language or conscious thought, it learned to scan tone, expression, expectation, and environment. That is how a nervous system learns to stay in relationship with the conditions it is born into. Awareness remained present throughout that learning. Attention simply learned to pass over it because attending elsewhere was more important.

I once worked with someone who described walking into a room at a party and immediately scanning faces—who looked welcoming, who looked annoyed, who might be safe to approach. She said it happened so fast she barely registered doing it. Her attention moved outward automatically, reading the room before she had even decided whether to stay.

She had been doing this her whole life. As a child, she learned to read her mother's mood the moment she walked in the door from work. Tense shoulders meant stay quiet. A soft smile meant it was safe to talk. That early learning shaped how her attention moved for decades. It was not a conscious choice. It was how she learned to stay connected and safe.

This is the human condition. Attention centers on what allows us to belong, remain intact, and make sense of what is happening around us. Over time, that orientation becomes familiar and automatic, and it begins to feel like who we are rather than how we learned to orient.

When awareness seems distant or inaccessible, it is not absent. Attention is simply following habit, protection, and what once carried meaning or necessity.

How Awareness Moves

Awareness is the capacity to notice what is happening—thoughts, emotions, physical sensations, impulses—without requiring that anything be changed or acted on. It simply registers what is here.

In that sense, awareness is receptive rather than effortful. It does not analyze, correct, or intervene. It allows experience to be seen as it is, before judgment, interpretation, or strategy begin shaping it.

The difficulty is not that we lack awareness. The difficulty is what happens the moment something becomes noticeable.

Almost immediately, criticism arrives. A habit is judged, a reaction is labeled, and an impulse is overridden quickly and automatically. Phase One does not ask for this to stop. It simply notices when it happens. That noticing is enough. Awareness does not force change. It creates space, and within that space experience reorganizes on its own.

What we call autopilot is patterned responsiveness. The nervous system learns what works to navigate situations efficiently, and repetition makes those responses swift and automatic. Awareness remains present throughout. It simply stops being the center of attention.

I once sat with someone who described being in a work meeting when a colleague made a dismissive comment. She felt her chest tighten, her face flush, and her mind immediately begin forming a defensive response. She did not decide to react. It happened before she could think about it. Her attention narrowed completely onto the comment—what it meant, what it implied, how she should respond.

It was not until later, walking back to her desk, that she realized she had been holding her breath for the last ten minutes of the meeting. Her jaw was tight. Her shoulders were lifted. Awareness arrived late, the way it often does, and with it came judgment: *Why do I always do this? Why can't I just let things go?*

What she noticed eventually noticed was the sequence. Attention narrowed in response to perceived threat. Meaning rushed in to organize the experience. Self-criticism followed as an attempt to regain control.

When she saw that sequence—not to stop it or correct it, but simply to recognize it—there was a brief widening. The experience itself did not change, but there was more space around it. That widening was awareness becoming visible again.

Awareness does not disappear when we react. It simply stops being what attention is organized around.

Recognition often arrives after the reaction—you notice yourself forming a defensive response before the other person has finished speaking, or realize you were bracing only once your body has already tightened. Early on, recognition frequently arrives in hindsight. Over time, the gap shortens.

Awareness does not reopen through force. It becomes visible again when attention settles, and the system senses that it does not need to perform or correct itself in order to be acceptable. The movement is simply to notice and return.

Relating to Awareness

Contact with awareness shifts many times throughout the day. The question is not whether awareness is present—you are aware. The question is how you relate to it when contact becomes more or less visible.

Many people assume the goal is to remain present as consistently as possible. So when attention narrows—as it does constantly, for everyone—it gets interpreted as a mistake. Something to correct. Something to push back against. That effort usually tightens the system further.

I once worked with someone who described a week where she had been trying to stay present throughout her days. She set reminders on her phone, paused to take deep breaths, and checked in with her body regularly. By the end of the week, she was exhausted.

"I'm trying so hard to be aware," she told me, "but I keep losing it. I feel like I'm failing at presence."

What she was encountering was the difference between maintaining awareness and relating to it. She had turned awareness into a task—something to achieve and sustain. When attention naturally narrowed, she interpreted it as failure and tried to force it back.

When she shifted from trying to maintain awareness to noticing when it felt close or distant, something eased. She stopped treating narrowing as a problem to fix. She began to recognize the moment awareness became visible again when contact returned.

The fluctuation was no longer evidence of failure. It was simply how attention moves.

Relating to awareness means allowing that movement. Some moments feel clear and grounded. Others feel scattered or distant. Both belong to ordinary experience.

When awareness is treated as something that must be sustained, fluctuation feels like failure. When it is treated as relational—something you are in contact with rather than something you possess—fluctuation becomes expected.

Awareness is not practiced to arrive somewhere. The practice is relationship: remaining in contact with experience as it unfolds, even when that experience includes distraction, judgment, or withdrawal.

A Practice of Noticing

This practice is not about creating a particular state or experience. You do not need to feel calm, focused, or present before beginning. The practice meets whatever is here — including distraction, restlessness, or uncertainty. Attention is not held in place. It is noticed, and contact is reestablished when it becomes clear that attention has moved.

The Practice

Settle into a position that feels reasonably comfortable. Let your body be supported.

Take a moment to notice that you are here. You might notice the weight of your body, the contact with the surface beneath you, or the rhythm of your breathing. There is nothing to control. Just notice what is already happening.

As you sit, awareness may feel clear or diffuse, steady or moving quickly from one thing to another.

You might notice thoughts moving through your mind, sensations in your body, emotions, or a lack of emotion. Rather than focusing on any one thing, let your attention rest lightly on the experience of noticing itself.

At some point, you may realize your attention has drifted — that you have been thinking, planning, remembering, or judging. When that happens, acknowledge it as a moment of recognition.

Gently allow your attention to return to whatever feels most immediate right now. This could be the breath, a bodily sensation, or the sense of being here. You may need to do this many times. Each time attention is noticed and allowed to return without force, you are practicing relationship rather than control.

If judgment arises about how the practice is going or about yourself, notice that too. Judgment is part of experience.

You may also notice moments of distance or numbness. If that happens, stay present with the sense of distance itself, without trying to change it. Awareness does not disappear when experience shifts. It changes how it shows up.

Let yourself move between noticing and drifting, contact and distance. There is no ideal rhythm. There is only what is happening.

When you are ready to end the practice, take a moment to notice how you feel — not to evaluate it, but to register it.

This orientation continues beyond the practice. Noticing when attention narrows. Noticing when awareness returns. No effort to maintain anything. Only a willingness to notice, again and again.

Living Awareness

As this phase begins to settle, attention often returns to the ordinary rhythms of life. The focus is no longer on understanding awareness or trying to hold it in place. What has been noticed does not need to be maintained.

Awareness was never something you created. It does not depend on effort, and it does not disappear when attention moves elsewhere. What changes is simply whether it sits in the foreground or the background of experience at a given moment.

In daily life, this appears in small ways. A reaction becomes visible as it happens. A familiar tension in the body is noticed without immediately trying to resolve it. Thoughts move through without carrying the same urgency to explain or control. Emotions appear sooner. Patterns become recognizable as they unfold rather than only in hindsight.

There is no requirement to constantly observe yourself. Awareness continues whether you think about it or not—in conversations, decisions, conflicts, routines, and quiet moments alone.

Living this phase is less about maintaining a state of awareness and more about developing a different relationship with your own adaptation. You begin to feel its intelligence, not just its constraint. The familiar pull toward vigilance appears, or the old habit of making yourself small becomes recognizable, and it is seen as a pattern with a history rather than a personal failing.

You may notice the loop beginning to run—the interpretation, the physical response, the impulse to act—and realize you are no longer entirely inside it. The pattern is still unfolding, but there is space around it. This is what it feels like to be in relationship with your own conditioning. It does not disappear, but you are no longer identical to it.

Awareness does not stabilize into a permanent state. It shifts with fatigue, stress, connection, and circumstance.

Some days feel clearer. Others feel automatic and fast again. Neither indicates progress nor regression. They simply reflect the changing conditions of being alive.

Over time, what was described in this phase becomes less something you remember and more something that accompanies experience. The sense that you must manage yourself softens. Reactions still happen. Discomfort still arises. Attention still narrows and widens.

The difference is often subtle. Experience is noticed more often while it is happening, and less energy is spent fighting what is already unfolding.

Life continues, and awareness remains present within it.

Chapter 14

The Phase of Unraveling

T he Phase of Unraveling doesn't arrive as clarity. It shows up as friction.

A familiar response that once felt automatic now feels slightly off. A role you've always played suddenly feels like acting. A story about who you are no longer quite fits, even though you can't name what's wrong with it. You start to say something you've said a thousand times — an explanation, an apology, a way of smoothing things over — and you pause mid-sentence, unsure why you're saying it. Or you find yourself in a situation that would normally trigger a predictable reaction, and instead, there's just hesitation. A gap between what you'd usually do and what feels true.

I used to panic when this happened. I thought the friction meant I was regressing, or doing something wrong. Now I understand it differently. The friction is the feeling of the walls coming down — and the walls coming down is exactly what's supposed to happen.

In The Phase of Awareness, we looked at how meaning forms. We adapt to the world we are given. Because we adapt, conditioning happens. And as conditioning happens, meaning forms — deep, foundational, and almost entirely without our consent. That unchosen meaning becomes the filter through which we experience everything.

Unraveling is what happens when that filter becomes visible.

Here is the thing worth knowing before we go any further: unraveling is not something you do to yourself. It is what happens when you begin to relate differently to what's already there. The same nervous system that adapted to survive also has an innate drive toward coherence. You don't have to force this process. Given the right conditions, it is as inevitable as the conditioning that preceded it.

The mechanism of Awareness was adaptation. The mechanism of Unraveling is relationship.

Awareness, on its own, allows things to soften. When you see conditioning as adaptation rather than defect, the fight with yourself begins to quiet. But relationship is what allows you to get your hands on what you are now aware of. To move it around. To look at it from different angles. To notice cause and effect. To interact with what was once just happening to you.

Unraveling is not dismantling. It is the act of turning toward what you've been avoiding, fused with, or carrying alone, and making contact with it. And as you make contact, things naturally begin to shift. The self that is oriented toward coherence emerges.

The Qualities of Being Human

Before we talk about what gets shaped, we need to talk about what does not.

You were born with something already in place. Beneath personality, behavior, and the identity that formed around your conditions, there is an essential nature that exists simply by virtue of being alive. This nature is not a single, static thing. It is a constellation of innate human qualities—the fundamental capacities that make you you.

These qualities were not developed or earned. They do not arrive later through insight or healing. They were present from the beginning, and they have never left.

The first of these qualities is inherent worth. This is easiest to see in very young children. A baby does not question their right to exist or measure their value through usefulness or performance. There is an unspoken dignity in their presence. They are complete exactly as they are.

Another quality is the capacity to feel, to reach, and to depend. A child cries when they need to, rests when they are tired, and reaches out when they want connection without negotiating whether they are allowed to take up space. This is vulnerability in its simplest form—the open state of being affected by the world and needing others.

Reaching is not weakness. It is the expression of our relational wiring. Feeling is not a problem to solve. It is the way life moves through us.

I once worked with someone who described watching her three-year-old daughter cry—the kind of crying that takes over the whole body. Her daughter had wanted a snack before dinner and had been told no, and the disappointment was immediate and total. She collapsed on the floor, wailing, her face red and her body shaking with the force of it.

What struck her was not the tantrum itself but what happened afterward. Within minutes, her daughter's crying slowed. She took a few shuddering breaths, wiped her face, and returned to playing with her toys.

There was no residue. No story about what the "no" meant about her worth or her mother's love. The feeling had moved through her completely, and then it was over.

She told me, "I realized I can't do that anymore. When I'm disappointed or hurt, I don't just feel it and let it go. I make it mean something. I replay it. I build a case about what it says about the other person or about me. I carry it for days."

Watching her daughter, she could see something she once had—the capacity to feel an experience fully without turning it into identity.

What she was recognizing was her own essential nature, the part of her that could still feel, still be affected, still move through experience before interpretation took over.

The final quality is wholeness—the recognition that these capacities of worth, feeling, reaching, and depending cannot actually be taken from you. They can be covered over, forgotten, or organized around so tightly that they become difficult to recognize, but they cannot be destroyed.

They remain present beneath the identities and protections that formed around them.

That is what this phase begins to uncover: how being human took shape within the conditions you were given, so that contact with what has always been intact can return—not through effort, but through recognition.

The Conditions of Being Human

We encounter life before we have the capacity to hold its impact. Before language, logic, or reflection, experience registers directly through the body. The nervous system absorbs what happens without explanation, and those impressions remain.

To be human is to arrive open and affected, dependent on others, and shaped by conditions we did not choose.

Even in the most loving environments, experience exceeds what can be fully held. Mismatch happens. Limits are reached. Caregivers bring their own nervous systems, their own histories, and their own constraints.

This is not an exception to the human condition. It is the human condition itself.

What follows—the adaptation, the protection, the identity that forms around vulnerability—is the natural result of being a learning organism inside an imperfect world.

The nervous system organizes itself around three unavoidable realities of being human: vulnerability, powerlessness, and the need for connection. How those realities were met shaped everything that followed.

Vulnerability

To be human is to live in relationship with vulnerability from the beginning.

Vulnerability is the condition of being affected—of being a body in the world that can be touched, changed, and influenced by what happens around it. Early in life, that openness is total. Children cannot regulate their own nervous systems, cannot leave unsafe situations, and cannot fully understand what is happening around them.

Your relationship to vulnerability was shaped by how it was received—whether it was met with safety and responsiveness or with dismissal, overwhelm, or silence.

I once sat with someone who described learning very early that crying was not welcome in her family. No one said this directly. Instead, whenever she cried, her father would leave the room while her mother would sigh and say, "You're fine. There's no reason to be upset."

The message became clear over time: vulnerability created distance.

If she wanted connection, she needed to be okay. By the time she reached adulthood, she could not cry in front of anyone. Even alone, tears felt dangerous, like opening a door she might not be able to close. She minimized her feelings before anyone else could. "I'm fine" became automatic. When sadness appeared, she redirected her attention, busied herself, or explained it away. Over time, she began to notice the cost. No one really knew when she was struggling. She was close to people, but only up to a point. Her relationship to vulnerability had become one of management and distance.

This is not a story about blame. It is a story about cause and effect. The nervous system learns. When vulnerability is met with distance, it learns to keep vulnerability at a distance. The relationship to the self organizes around the relationship that was first modeled. That organization remains long after the original conditions have passed, until a different kind of relationship becomes possible.

Powerlessness

To be human is also to live in relationship with powerlessness.

Powerlessness is the condition of dependence. For a time, survival depends entirely on others. Children cannot meet their own needs, alter their circumstances, or make the world be what they need it to be.

Your relationship to powerlessness was shaped by how it was met—whether dependence was supported or whether it unfolded within chaos, neglect, or inconsistency.

I once worked with someone who described how difficult it was for him to ask for help. Even when collaboration made obvious sense, he insisted on doing everything himself. At work, he took on projects that required a team. At home, he refused help from his partner even when he was overwhelmed. Asking felt like weakness.

When we explored the source of that feeling, he remembered growing up in a chaotic household. His parents were unpredictable—sometimes available, sometimes absent. If he needed something, he could not count on them to show up. So he stopped needing.

He learned to do things himself, stay under the radar, and rely only on his own effort. As an adult, that pattern continued. Dependence felt unsafe. Self-sufficiency became the only reliable form of control. The cost was isolation.

This is not a story about what went wrong. It is a story about what was learned. When dependence is unsafe, the nervous system learns to be self-sufficient. The relationship to the self organizes around the need not to need. That organization remains long after the original conditions have passed, until a different relationship becomes possible.

Connection

To be human is to live in relationship with the need for connection.

Connection is biological. When it is reliable and attuned, it supports regulation and the development of a coherent sense of self. When it is inconsistent, rejecting, or overwhelming, distance becomes a form of protection.

Your relationship to connection was shaped by how it was met.

I once worked with someone who described feeling as though she had two versions of herself. One was the version people saw—competent, warm, easy to be around. The other was the version she kept private—anxious, uncertain, full of doubt. She never let anyone see that second version.

As we explored this, she recognized that the split had formed early. Her mother was emotionally fragile, and when she was upset as a child, her mother would become even more upset. She quickly learned that expressing her own needs created more instability. So she became the easy child.

She learned to keep her real feelings to herself and take care of the emotional atmosphere around her. As an adult, that pattern continued. She was close to people, but only the parts of herself she felt safe showing. The rest stayed hidden. She often felt lonely, even in relationships, because no one really knew her.

This is not a story about a broken self. It is a story about a divided one. When connection is conditional, the nervous system learns to meet the conditions. The relationship to the self organizes around what is permitted. That organization remains long after the original conditions have passed, until a different kind of relationship becomes possible.

Pause and Notice: The Shape of Your Conditions

Before moving forward, take a moment to let this settle.

You do not need to analyze your childhood or construct a narrative about what happened. Simply notice the atmosphere of your early life—the tone of it. What it felt like to be vulnerable in the environment you grew up in. Whether powerlessness was met with support or with something harder. Whether connection felt reliable, conditional, or uncertain.

You might notice a role that formed early—the responsible one, the easy one, the strong one, the quiet one, the helper, the peacekeeper.

If a role comes to mind, stay with it gently. Notice what it allowed. Notice what it required. See if you can sense how it formed around something intact—around belonging that needed shape in order to remain possible.

You are not looking for a full story. You are noticing structure. The shape of your conditions.

If nothing appears, stay with that. The absence of clarity is also information.

How Experience is Held in Relationship

We do not learn to feel on our own.

The capacity is there from the beginning—to be moved, to feel intensely, to return to ourselves after distress. But early access to that capacity depends on another person. It depends on someone who can remain steady while experience moves through us, someone who stays present rather than leaving us alone with what we are carrying.

This is more than a developmental stage. It becomes the original template for how we learn to relate to our own inner lives. The way others respond to our experience gradually becomes the way we respond to it ourselves.

When a baby is distressed and a caregiver responds—not by removing the distress but by staying present with it—something is learned that no one explicitly teaches. The body registers that intensity can move, that connection does not disappear when emotion appears, and that it is possible to feel something fully without being abandoned inside it.

Through these repeated moments of being met, the nervous system learns something it will carry for the rest of its life: experience can be held, and holding it does not require being alone.

When that accompaniment is consistent, the relationship to emotional life often remains more available. Feelings can unfold within connection. Distress does not have to be managed or minimized before it is allowed to exist. The body learns that experience moves through us rather than something we must contain by ourselves.

When accompaniment is inconsistent, unavailable, or unsafe, the nervous system organizes differently. Suppression appears. Vigilance increases. Control becomes important. The habit of taking things to your room and waiting until they pass takes shape.

These responses are not signs that something broke. They are what any intelligent system does when conditions change: reorganizing around what is available. And when accompaniment is not available, what becomes available is the capacity to carry things alone.

I once worked with someone who described a quality of silence he had carried for most of his life. Not a comfortable silence, but a managed one—the kind that required effort to maintain. When he was a child, his household was unpredictable. Strong emotion rarely settled things; it tended to escalate them. He learned early that the safest response when he felt something intensely was to go quiet. He would take the feeling to his room and wait for it to pass.

By the time he was an adult, this had become automatic. He was thoughtful, contained, and easy to be around. People often described him as calm. Yet inside, he was carrying things alone that he had no idea how to bring into contact with another person.

When his partner asked how he was feeling, he would answer. But the answer was always slightly beside the point. The real thing stayed back—not because he was withholding, but because he had never learned that it was safe to bring it forward.

What eventually changed was not a skill he developed but an experience he began having repeatedly: bringing something real into contact with another person and finding that it was received without urgency, correction, or pressure to resolve it. His system began to learn something it had missed the first time—that experience could be held in relationship, that he did not have to carry it alone.

What changes in moments like these is access, not capacity. The ability to feel, to be moved, and to recover does not disappear when accompaniment is absent. It reorganizes around protection. Experience becomes something carried privately in ways that preserve functioning even when connection is not there to help hold it.

This is why so much unraveling takes place in relationship. Relationship is the original context in which access formed. When experience is met without being fixed—when it can be stayed with rather than managed—the nervous system no longer has to carry intensity alone.

Access returns because the conditions that required protection have changed.

The essential nature—the connected, intact quality of being human—was never removed. It was protected. And when relationship becomes available again, internally or externally, experience no longer has to be carried in isolation.

Pause and Notice: How Experience Was Met

Let your attention drift back—not toward a specific memory but toward the atmosphere of your early emotional life.

What was it like to feel something intensely as a child?

You may not recall a particular event. Instead, you might sense tone: how sadness was received, how fear was responded to, what happened when anger appeared, or when you needed comfort.

Notice whether emotion was accompanied or whether it was something you learned to carry alone.

Stay with the felt sense rather than an explanation. You are not looking for a story or a conclusion. You are noticing the quality of how experience was held—or how you learned to hold it yourself when no one else could.

There is nothing to solve here. Only something to notice.

How We Learn Who to Be

The nervous system does not only learn how to hold experience. It also learns who to be.

As the body absorbs the conditions of its environment—what brings closeness and what creates distance, what is welcomed and what overwhelms—it begins drawing conclusions that reach beyond how emotion is managed. It begins to register which version of the self is safe to bring forward.

We learn which feelings are welcome and which must remain hidden, which needs can be expressed and which are better swallowed, which parts of ourselves can appear without threatening connection, and which ones have to wait.

These conclusions do not form as decisions. They settle gradually as patterns of attention, response, and self-presentation that become familiar ways of being. Over time, those patterns stop feeling like adaptations and start feeling like the self.

From these adaptations, certain parts of the self take on specific roles—to preserve connection, manage vulnerability, or maintain stability. The responsible one. The easy one. The strong one. The quiet one. The helper. The peacekeeper.

These roles are not problems. They are expressions of intelligence—ways the system found to remain intact when the conditions of being human exceeded what could easily be held.

They formed around something real: around worth that could not be felt directly and so had to be demonstrated, around belonging that required a particular shape in order to remain possible, around connection that could only be maintained when certain parts of the self stayed out of sight.

These roles became the original terms of your relationship with yourself. They determined which parts of you were allowed into the relationship and which parts had to be set aside to maintain connection.

Identity, as it is used here, does not describe who you are. It describes how your system learned to organize its relationship with itself in response to the conditions it encountered.

Pause and Notice: How You Learned Who to Be

Let your attention settle on the roles that may have formed early in your life. There is no need to analyze them. Simply recognize them.

Was there a version of you that felt necessary—the responsible one, the easy one, the strong one, the quiet one, the helper, the peacekeeper?

If a role comes to mind, stay with it gently. Notice what it allowed. Notice what it required.

See if you can sense how it formed around something intact—around worth that could not be felt directly, around belonging that needed shape in order to remain accessible.

You are not looking for a full story. You are noticing structure.

If nothing appears, stay with that. The absence of clarity is also information.

This is the architecture of your survival. It is not a list of flaws or a catalog of things you need to fix. It is the shape your system took to ensure you could remain in connection with the world around you. Before you try to change any of it, just let it be true. You learned to be who you needed to be. It worked.

When Protection Becomes Identity

At some point, protection stops feeling like something you do and begins to feel like who you are.

This shift does not happen through decision. It emerges through repetition, as patterns become so familiar they stop registering as patterns at all. Vigilance, self-sufficiency, performance, withdrawal—each of these once arose in response to specific conditions. They appeared because those conditions required them.

Over time, the nervous system begins to anticipate rather than wait. The response arrives before the moment itself, guided by what was once necessary for survival.

Somewhere within that repetition, the adaptation becomes the story. You are the responsible one. You are the one who does not need help. You are the one who keeps everything together. You are the one who stays quiet to keep the peace. Not because you consciously chose to be, but because the pattern repeated often enough that it became the lens through which you understand yourself.

This is the moment when you are no longer in relationship with your protection. You are fused with it.

To be in relationship with something requires two—you, and the thing you are relating to. When protection and identity fuse, there is only one. There is just you being the responsible one, not needing help, keeping everything together.

Protection stops appearing as a strategy and begins to appear as the self.

When that fusion occurs, the parts of you that the protection formed to manage become distant. The vulnerable part. The needy part. The angry part. The uncertain part. To be fused with the competent part means being distant from the part that feels incompetent. To be fused with strength means being distant from weakness.

The fusion itself creates the division.

Protection is doing its job. Internally, it organizes the self around which parts would disrupt connection if they appeared. Externally, it presents the version of the self that keeps connection possible. It is not a false self. It is a functional one—the part that learned how to navigate the relational environment you were in.

I once worked with someone who described herself as low-maintenance. She did not ask for much. She handled her own feelings. She was the steady one in every room.

Growing up, strong emotions made her family uncomfortable. When she cried, the atmosphere tightened. When she was angry, she was told she was overreacting. No one was intentionally harsh, but there was little room for intensity. So she adapted.

The part of her that felt afraid quieted. The part that needed comfort became self-sufficient. The part that longed for reassurance learned to anticipate others instead.

Nothing in her broke. But her experience divided.

As an adult, she appeared capable and independent. Yet when she was overwhelmed, she went blank. When she was hurt, she minimized it. She had relationships, but she often felt alone inside them. The competent part led. The vulnerable part remained out of sight.

She was not in relationship with her competence. She was fused with it. And because she was fused with it, she could not be in relationship with the parts of herself that felt overwhelmed or needed support. Those parts were still there. They were simply kept out of sight, and maintaining that distance required an enormous amount of energy.

She came in wanting to fix the blankness, the minimizing, the loneliness inside relationships. She had tried for years. What she had not tried was looking at any of it as something other than a problem.

When she began to sit with the blankness and ask what it had once been for, rather than how to make it stop, the quality of her relationship with herself began to shift. She moved from being fused with competence to being in relationship with the parts it had been protecting. The parts she had been fighting started to feel less like failures and more like responses that once made complete sense.

The nervous system does not produce dysfunction. It produces protection. What we often call pathology is protection that has outlived its context.

This is the hinge of the entire process. As long as you experience the protection as who you are—as long as you are fused with the competence, the anxiety, the withdrawal, or the performance—nothing about it can truly change. At best, it can be managed. The effort becomes trying to be a better version of the adaptation itself.

Something shifts the moment that identification loosens. When you begin to see the protection not as who you are, but as something your system learned to do on your behalf, a small space appears. Anxiety is no longer identical to you; it is something you are experiencing. Competence is no longer your identity; it is something you once developed in order to survive.

Within that space, relationship becomes possible again.

Pause and Notice: Recognizing Protection as Intelligence

Bring to mind a protective response you know well—something familiar, something you may have judged or tried to outgrow.

Stay with the felt sense of it. Notice where it lives in your body. Notice its pace. Notice what it seems oriented toward.

See if you can sense that it formed in response to something—that it once served as an intelligent adjustment to conditions.

What might it have been protecting? What would have been exposed without it?

Notice what shifts, if anything, when you regard this part as something that once made sense.

You are not required to feel compassion for it. You are not required to approve of it.

Only to recognize that it served a purpose.

Stay here for a moment. Let the recognition settle. You do not need to figure out what to do with this part of yourself yet. The work right now is simply allowing it to exist as a response rather than a failure. Just let it be here.

If that recognition feels distant, notice that too. Even distance has a shape.

The Relationship You're Already In

You are already in relationship with all of this—with vulnerability, with power, with connection, with the roles you learned to play, with the protection that became identity. It is not a relationship you chose, but it is the one you are in.

The first half of this chapter was about seeing that relationship more clearly: how it formed, the logic that holds it in place, the cost of maintaining it. The rest of this phase turns toward something else. Not fixing it. Not healing it. Not managing it more effectively. But making contact with what is already here. It means turning toward the parts of yourself you have been fused with, avoiding, or carrying alone, and beginning to relate to them as something other than a problem.

This is the pivot—from seeing what formed to relating with what is. Change happens through relationship. The rest of this phase is about what that actually means.

How to Be in Relationship

What does it mean to be in relationship with these parts of yourself? How do you do it?

The answer is not a technique so much as an orientation, and that orientation begins with recognizing what is already here. Three things do not come and go: your essential nature, awareness, and capacity. Your essential nature—the wholeness, worth, and dignity you were born with—was never taken from you. It was only covered over. Awareness, the capacity to notice what is happening without immediately collapsing into judgment, has been present in every moment, even when attention was fused with a story. Capacity, the ability to feel, to be moved, and to recover, was never lost. It was organized around protection.

These three are the ground. They remain true no matter what is happening in the foreground of experience. They do not drift. What drifts is access.

Access is the relationship. It is the quality of your contact with what is already here. When access is open, you feel connected to your own wholeness. Awareness is easier to rest in. Capacity feels available. When access narrows, you feel disconnected, fused with a story, convinced your capacity is gone. But the ground itself has not disappeared. What has shifted is your felt contact with it.

For a long time, your orientation has been outward. As we saw in Phase One, attention learned early to scan the environment, read the room, and organize around what was needed for safety and connection. That outward movement was a brilliant adaptation. It is also what makes the ground beneath you harder to feel.

The shift, then, is inward. Not inward to fix or manage what is there, but inward to make contact with it. It is the movement of attention from what is happening out there to what is happening here. The quality of that attention matters. It is not demanding, not corrective, not trying to get anywhere. It is simply present.

That is what it means to be in relationship. You feel a familiar tightness in your chest and, instead of distracting yourself, you place a hand there. You hear the inner critic and, instead of arguing with it, you become curious about what it fears. You notice you are judging yourself and, instead of turning the judgment into another problem, you simply notice that it is here.

You are turning toward rather than away. You are making contact.

The Practice: Staying With a Protective Part

This practice is an invitation to do something most of us have rarely tried: to turn toward a protective part of ourselves without trying to change it.

Not to fix it. Not to fully understand it. Not to negotiate with it or convince it of anything. Just to stay with it—to bring your attention toward it and remain there, as a presence alongside it rather than a force against it.

This is what it means to be in relationship with protection rather than fused with it. In practice, it is much simpler than it sounds. The difficulty is not the method. The difficulty is the habit of opposition, the long-standing tendency to treat these parts as problems to solve rather than as responses that formed for a reason and have been carrying something ever since.

Begin by choosing one part.

Begin with one part. You do not need to work with all of them at once. Choose one that feels familiar: the part that gets defensive when you feel criticized, the part that shuts down when things become emotionally intense, the part that over-explains, over-functions, disappears, stays busy, or scans for what might go wrong.

You will recognize it by its familiarity. It is the one that returns reliably, the one you have probably tried to manage or get rid of, the one with a tone or quality you already know.

Find a position that feels supportive and let your attention settle. There is no need to close your eyes if that feels uncomfortable. Just allow attention to move inward—not to search, but to arrive.

When you feel relatively settled, bring your attention toward the part you chose. You do not need to summon it or construct it. It is already here. You are only turning toward it.

Notice how it shows up. It may appear as a sensation in the body—a tightening in the chest, weight in the shoulders, restlessness in the legs. It may come as a voice, a tone, a posture, or a general felt presence without a clear shape. You do not need a clear image or a story. Let it be as it is.

Then stay with it.

That is the practice. Not analyzing it. Not asking it to explain itself. Not trying to soften it or move beyond it. Just staying.

As you remain present, notice what it is like to be here with this part. Where does it live most clearly in your body? How much space does it seem to take? Does it move quickly, or settle when attention arrives?

Notice what happens in you as you stay.

Does your attention tighten, soften, drift? Do you feel pulled to understand, reassure, or distance yourself? Let those movements be included in awareness without trying to manage them. They, too, are part of what is here.

If it feels natural, you might gently wonder what this part is oriented toward. What does it seem concerned about? What is it trying to manage? These questions are a way of remaining curious without becoming oppositional. You are not interrogating it. You are noticing it.

If nothing comes, stay with that. Silence, blankness, or a sense that nothing is happening are also expressions of protection. There is no correct way for this to unfold. Staying is enough.

From where you are now, allow a response to arise. Not a response that reassures, instructs, or reorients the part, but the simple fact of your presence alongside it. Steadiness. Availability. The quality of not requiring it to be different.

If words arise, let them remain minimal. If no words arise, let the response stay felt rather than spoken—a quality of accompaniment rather than a statement.

Let the contact settle.

Remain here for a few moments and notice what happens when protection is met without judgment or demand. You may notice softening. You may notice emotion moving. You may notice tension, distance, or no change at all. None of this needs to mean anything. The absence of change is not a problem. The presence of change is not a conclusion.

If it feels natural, notice what it is like for this part and your present awareness to exist together, neither leading, neither retreating.

This is often how change first appears. Not as transformation, but as contact. The pattern remains, but its authority shifts. What once felt like identity begins to feel like movement.

Unraveling unfolds when what was formed in isolation is met in relationship. As protection encounters steadiness rather than opposition, something beneath it becomes more accessible—not because it was created, but because it was never gone. The task from here is not to hold onto these moments, but to keep recognizing them.

Protection will still arise. Vulnerability will still surface. What changes is whether they have to carry experience alone.

When Access Narrows

There will be weeks when this feels close and weeks when it feels as though it was never there.

Familiar reactions return. Old patterns resurface. Practices that once felt available feel harder to approach. And the temptation—the very human temptation—is to read this as going backward.

It is not.

Access to awareness and essential nature does not open once and stay open. It widens and narrows in response to conditions. When the system senses safety, contact is easier. When it senses uncertainty or threat, protection shapes experience again. This is not regression. It is the same intelligence that learned to adapt still doing what it learned to do.

What often gets called resistance is protection recalibrating. As access widens, experiences once held at a distance—sensation, emotion, memory, vulnerability—begin to move closer. When that happens, protection responds quickly, not to interrupt the process, but to prevent overwhelm.

The response is often subtle. Attention drifts. Motivation thins. Doubt appears. Practices that once felt natural start to feel effortful.

None of this means something essential has been lost. Wholeness remains intact. What changes is access, narrowing in response to perceived risk and guided by the same intelligence that has always been trying to keep you safe.

A client once described feeling as though she was back at the beginning after a week of greater openness. She found herself irritated, avoidant, forgetting the practices, doubting the whole thing. When we stayed close to what had changed in her life that week—less sleep, more demands, an unnamed relational strain—the narrowing made immediate sense. Her system had recalibrated around volume and speed.

The return of old patterns had not erased what had been touched. It revealed what her nervous system still did when conditions tightened. When she stopped treating the narrowing as a problem, something in her settled. The urgency eased. Access returned almost incidentally.

Access does not widen through force. It widens through relationship. When narrowing is met with recognition rather than alarm, the system receives different information. Protection no longer has to work alone.

Unraveling is not linear. Access widens. Access narrows. Awareness remains present throughout. What changes is how safely the system can remain in contact as experience deepens.

Nothing needs to be forced open. The work continues through remaining in relationship with whatever appears, including the moments when access feels far away.

The Grief That Has No Story

Grief often arrives before you have a name for it.

Not the grief that comes with a clear loss—a death, an ending, something you can point to. This grief is quieter than that. It appears as heaviness, fatigue, or an ache moving through the body without attaching to anything specific. Nothing obvious has happened. And yet something is moving, and it carries the weight of grief.

This is often what it feels like when what was once carried alone is finally met.

The parts of yourself that have been managing, explaining, and holding everything together—when they begin to be accompanied rather than left to work in isolation—something releases. Not all at once. Not in a dramatic way. But the body knows the difference between being alone with something and being in relationship with it. And when that difference is felt, grief is often what moves through.

Not because something went wrong. Because something is finally being held.

Sometimes what is grieved is not the past itself, but the meanings that once organized experience. The belief that clarity would bring rest. That insight would resolve tension. That a fuller understanding of yourself would eventually deliver a stable sense of arrival. These are not small beliefs. Many people build entire lives around them. As they loosen, what they once promised falls away. That absence registers as loss, even when what is loosening was never actually working.

There may also be grief for identities that once provided coherence, even when they were constraining. The responsible one. The capable one. The one who does not need much. The one who always knows what to do. These roles carried structure. They organized movement through the world. As attachment to them loosens, the space that remains can feel unfamiliar, exposed in a way that is difficult to name, like standing in a room after the furniture has been moved.

I once worked with someone who described a strange flatness after years of living inside constant explanation. She kept waiting for the familiar sense of herself to return—the one who understood, interpreted, and stayed oriented through insight—but it did not. Instead there were stretches of quiet where experience felt almost featureless: making coffee, answering emails, walking the dog, a vague ache without a name.

Without the usual commentary, she felt unrecognizable to herself and assumed something had gone wrong.

What became clear was that it was not her experience that had flattened, but the identity that had once organized it. The part of her that made meaning quickly, that secured coherence through understanding, had loosened its grip. Without it, there was a period of disorientation. Life no longer arranged itself around who she was being or what it meant about her.

The grief that followed was not grief for the past itself. It was grief for the loss of a familiar way of knowing who she was.

She stayed with that disorientation longer than felt comfortable. What she found on the other side was not a new story, but a way of being present to experience before it had already been organized into meaning. Life felt less explained. It also felt more immediate. More hers.

Meaning had not disappeared. Identity had begun to unravel, making room for experience to be lived before it was explained.

For those accustomed to knowing themselves through story, this pause can feel unsettling. What dissolves is not meaning itself, but the compulsion to decide what experience means before it has been fully lived. Life may feel flatter or less articulated for a time—a pause in interpretation where meaning is no longer placed ahead of contact.

Wholeness remains intact throughout. What changes is how much experience must be explained, secured, or resolved in order to feel permissible. Grief appears as the structures that once held life together begin to loosen. And as they do, something truer starts organizing itself through lived presence rather than through the story of who you have been.

Living Unraveling

Things do not necessarily feel clearer as this phase enters daily life. At times, they feel less certain. A familiar role feels tighter than it used to. A response that once seemed natural now carries a sense of strain. You may notice yourself pausing in situations where you once moved quickly—not because you have found a better response, but because the automatic one no longer fires in quite the same way.

That pause can be disorienting. It can feel like something is wrong.

Nothing is wrong. The pattern is still there. What has changed is the fusion.

For a long time, the primary relationship was with the patterns themselves. You were fused with the anxiety, the responsibility, the story. There was no space between I *am* and I *feel*. As that fusion begins to loosen, a space opens. It is not detachment. It is a different kind of intimacy.

You are not the sadness. You are with the sadness. You are not the anger. You are with the anger. Experience can be held without being identical to it.

This is what reorganization feels like from the inside. Some situations will still pull you straight into familiar territory. Others will feel different—more open, more unsettled, less certain about how they are supposed to go. You may feel the impulse to accommodate, withdraw, or control while also sensing that another response might be possible.

Sometimes you follow the familiar path. Sometimes you do not. Both belong to the process.

There can also be fatigue. Identity has been carrying effort for a long time, often invisibly—the effort of maintaining a particular version of yourself, of staying oriented through a story about who you are. As that effort eases, the system sometimes needs a break. Confusion, uncertainty, and emotional fluctuation are not signs that something is failing. They are often what it feels like when the inner world is settling into a different kind of order.

And something else becomes possible there. When you are no longer fused with the pattern, you become more available to be known. Not the version of yourself the pattern presents—the capable one, the composed one, the one who has it together—but the actual you, with the actual experience you are having.

Other people can feel the difference. There is something in genuine contact that cannot be performed. When the fusion loosens, contact becomes real, and being seen stops feeling dangerous and begins to feel like what relationship was always for.

Clarity tends to arrive gradually and from the side. Not as a new identity replacing the old one, but as a change in what experience must organize itself around. The need to hold yourself together in a particular way softens. Responses become less forced. Needs become easier to sense, even when they are not yet easy to speak.

Chapter 15

The Phase of Emerging

The Phase of Emerging is not about suddenly knowing what you want or having the confidence to go after it. It's quieter than that. It's the moment you're halfway through an email, and you delete the long explanation you were writing, and simply say what you need to say.

It's noticing you're tired and canceling plans, and the guilt you expected to feel just isn't there. Or it's there, but it's softer, and the need for rest is louder.

It's being in a conversation and feeling a familiar pull to agree with something that doesn't feel true, and instead, you just stay quiet. You don't argue. You don't correct. You just don't abandon yourself. And the silence that follows feels more honest than the agreement would have.

This phase is about the emergence of Agency. Agency is not the same as choice. Choice is a cognitive act. Agency is a somatic state. It's the capacity of the nervous system to respond from a place of wholeness and presence, rather than from a place of conditioned adaptation. It's what becomes available when access to capacity is present.

In early development, we lack agency because we are dependent. Our survival depends on adaptation. As adults, we have the potential for agency, but it's often obscured by the very adaptations that got us through childhood.

The Phase of Awareness was about seeing those adaptations. The Phase of Unraveling was about beginning to be in relationship with them. The Phase of Emerging is about what happens when that relationship deepens: agency, which was always present but inaccessible, begins to emerge.

As access to wholeness becomes more reliable, a different organization takes the lead—one that can stay with discomfort, allow impact without immediately moving into control, and remain in contact without hardening or disappearing. Response does not have to precede choice. There is more space between sensation and reaction. This space does not require effort. It appears as the nervous system registers that it can remain intact while staying present. Within that space, choice becomes possible again.

Agency, then, is not the ability to make correct decisions. It is access to the capacity to remain with experience long enough to feel what is actually happening before responding. It is the return of choice, not as a strategy, but as a natural consequence of restored access to the self.

The Language That Was Always There

In The Phase of Unraveling, we learned to be in relationship with the adaptations that once helped us survive. As that relationship deepens, the energy previously used to manage, suppress, and override our own experience begins to loosen. What returns in that space is agency. Agency is not a new skill that must be learned. It is the re-emergence of an inherent human capacity—the ability to feel, to know, and to respond from a place that is not organized entirely around protection.

This restored capacity has a language. It is not a language of words, but of bodily experience. It speaks through the signal of our values, the biological reality of our needs, and the protective intelligence of our boundaries. Where survival once required learning the rules of others, agency introduces a different orientation. We begin to listen to the language of our own system. This is not a movement toward selfishness. It is a return to the self—the ground from which genuine connection becomes possible.

What Sustains You

Needs sustain a human being. They are the biological force that keeps life moving. To be a living body is to have them. This is not a story or a weakness. It is the simple, non-negotiable reality of being alive.

For a long time, your needs may have been organized around adaptation and survival. You may have learned that they threatened connection, that they were inconvenient, excessive, or dangerous. An intelligent system learned to ignore them, override them, or abandon them in the service of staying attached. This was not a mistake. It was a brilliant survival strategy.

As access to your wholeness widens and the system is no longer organized solely around survival, needs begin to emerge again. The desires of the vulnerable wholeness within you become perceptible. The capacity that appears in this phase allows you to feel those needs without being overwhelmed by them. The question is no longer whether you have needs. The question is whether you can hear them when they speak.

How Needs Are Recognized

The voice of dependency speaks through sensation. When we need something, the body registers it first. Because many of us learned to orient away from our own needs and instead organize ourselves around the needs of the environment, it can take time to recognize what a need actually feels like once it has gone unheard for too long.

Needs often appear indirectly. Loneliness signals a need for connection. Emptiness can signal a need for meaning or purpose. Depletion and burnout point toward a need for rest. A diffuse sense of lack may indicate that something essential for safety or nourishment is missing. Each is a different expression of the same reality: a part of you is unfed.

When these sensations appear, a need is trying to come into contact with awareness. With the return of capacity, there is space to hear that signal and remain with it rather than immediately overriding it. Agency creates that pause. Instead of moving instantly toward fixing or orienting outward again, there is room to decide how to respond.

I once worked with a woman who described years of pushing through fatigue. She would wake up tired, move through the day on momentum, and collapse at night, only to repeat the cycle the next morning. Rest was something she planned to get to eventually—after the project was finished, after the children were older, after life finally settled down.

One morning, she woke up and could not get out of bed. Not because she was sick. Not because she was depressed. Her body had simply stopped cooperating with the plan.

At first, she panicked. There were responsibilities waiting. People depended on her. She felt she could not afford to stop. But as she lay there, she noticed something unexpected. Her body was not asking permission. It was already resting. The real question was whether she would fight it.

She stayed in bed. She canceled her morning meetings. She did not check email, or strategize about how she would catch up later. She simply rested.

What surprised her most was the resistance that surfaced—guilt, anxiety, the familiar internal voice accusing her of laziness and irresponsibility. Beneath the resistance was relief. Her body had been asking for rest for months, perhaps years. She had simply become too practiced at overriding the signal to recognize it.

The need had always been present. What changed was her willingness to recognize it as legitimate, as information rather than failure.

What It Feels Like to Feel Your Needs

As you begin to hear the felt sense of your needs without immediately recoiling from them, others may surface as well—the need for touch, the need for play, the need for beauty, the need to be seen in your wholeness. These are not new needs. They are needs that were once too vulnerable to feel when the system was organized primarily around survival.

Their arrival can be disorienting. It can seem as though you are becoming more demanding or more dependent. You are not. You are becoming more alive. The landscape of your inner world expands. There is more of you present to be in relationship with. This is the emergence of vitality.

I once worked with a man who had built his life around being the one who was always fine. He was the steady friend, the reliable colleague, the person who never asked for anything. One afternoon, while recovering from a minor cold, he found himself overcome with a simple but startling desire: he wanted someone to bring him a bowl of soup.

The intensity of the feeling surprised him. It was not really about the soup. It was a deeper longing to be cared for, to briefly allow himself to depend on someone else. His first reaction was shame. A voice immediately appeared: *You're being pathetic. Get it yourself.*

But as he stayed with the sensation, something became clear. The feeling was not weakness. It was a sign of life. It was a need that had been buried for decades finally emerging into a space safe enough to feel it.

He did not ask for the soup. That was not the point, not yet. The point was that he allowed himself to feel the wanting of it. In doing so, he made contact with a part of himself he had long believed was gone.

Dependency in Relationship

Once a need becomes visible, a choice point appears. Some needs can be met alone. The need for rest can be met by canceling meetings and staying in bed. Hunger can be met by walking into the kitchen. But some needs cannot be fulfilled in isolation. Connection, care, comfort, and recognition exist within relationship.

Reaching is the embodied act of expressing a need to another person. It is the living expression of the capacity to feel, reach, and depend that began to return in the previous phase. For a long time, reaching may have felt too dangerous. The risk of being unmet, shamed, or abandoned in your need was too great. The system protected itself by not asking, not showing, not needing.

As agency emerges, that risk begins to change. The change is not that others will always respond or that every need will be met. Needs will still sometimes go unanswered. What shifts is that you can remain with your own experience when that happens. You can feel disappointment or sadness without abandoning yourself in response. This becomes the real ground of safety.

And when reaching is met—when someone listens, turns toward you, or brings the bowl of soup—the experience lands deeply. The need itself is met, but something else happens as well: the person beneath the need is met. Connection deepens. The nervous system settles. There is a sense of coherence, of rightness, of coming home to yourself in the presence of another. This is the experience of being human together.

I once worked with a man who was struggling in his marriage. His wife had grown distant over several months, and he found himself caught in a familiar pattern of trying to repair the distance—suggesting date nights, asking what was wrong, attempting to be a better partner. The more he tried, the further she seemed to pull away.

One evening after another tense dinner, he felt the familiar impulse to try again. This time, though, he paused. He noticed the loneliness. The fear that she might leave. Beneath both was a simple longing for her to turn toward him.

He knew he could not make that happen. All he could do was speak from where he actually was.

He walked into the living room where she was reading and stood quietly near the door.

"I feel really far away from you," he said. "And I'm scared."

She looked up from her book but did not respond immediately. He could feel the old panic rising—the urge to fill the silence, soften what he had said, make everything okay again. Instead, he stayed where he was.

Finally, she closed the book.

"I feel far away, too," she said.

It was not a solution. It was not a promise that everything would be fixed. But it was contact. For the first time in months, they were in the same room, feeling the same thing together. He had reached, and she had reached back.

Pause and Notice: Sensing What Is Needed

Bring your attention to your body and notice the landscape of sensation. Perhaps there is a place that feels tight, another that feels numb, another that feels relatively at ease. Nothing needs to change. Just notice what is present.

Is there a subtle pull toward something—a desire to stretch, close your eyes, look out the window, or take a deeper breath? These are impulses of the nervous system seeking regulation.

You may notice thirst, hunger, or the need to use the bathroom. These are basic needs we often ignore without realizing it. See if you can meet them simply.

You might also notice something more subtle: a need for quiet, connection, laughter, or rest. You do not need to know how those needs will be met right now. Just allow yourself to feel that they are there.

What is needed in this moment?

Not what you think you should need. Not what someone else might need.

What does your body, in its own intelligence, know that it needs?

Stay with the question and allow the answer to arise from the inside out.

The Keepers of the Self

There is a human instinct to protect what is precious. Once access to your own essential nature becomes more available, that instinct begins to organize around your own wholeness. A boundary is what that protection looks like in practice. It is not a wall built to keep the world out. It is the way your system gives the self a shape. In this sense, boundaries are the keepers of the self protecting, the integrity of what is already whole.

This is an expression of agency. For a long time, protection was organized around survival—around staying acceptable, managing the expectations of others, and preventing the loss of connection. As agency begins to return, protection reorganizes itself. It is no longer structured only around avoiding harm. It begins to organize around what is true. A boundary is the natural expression of a system that is no longer willing to abandon itself in order to belong.

The how of this is not a technique. It is an orientation. It is the turning of attention from what is happening outside of you to what is happening within. Not to fix it, not to manage it, but simply to make contact with it. It is the act of bringing a quality of attention to your inner world that is not demanding, not judging, and not trying to get anywhere. Just present.

The Shape of Your Presence

When protection begins to organize around wholeness, it first appears as a feeling. Sometimes that feeling is anger or resentment. These emotions often signal that your own integrity needs protecting—that a line has been crossed, or that a "yes" was given where a "no" was true.

At other times, the signal is shame. Shame often appears when you feel you have harmed someone else or failed to live in alignment with what matters to you. Both emotions are orienting. They are part of the body's way of telling you where a boundary exists, or where one was needed.

Resentment, in particular, is a remarkably loyal emotion. It consistently points to the places where you abandoned yourself to preserve connection or keep the peace. When resentment is understood as information rather than as a problem, it becomes a compass, guiding you back to the moment where your system registered a threat to its own integrity.

I once worked with a woman who had become the designated planner in her family. Every holiday, every birthday, every vacation—she was the one who made it happen. She was skilled at it, and everyone relied on her. For years, she told herself she didn't mind. Yet she came to see me because of a persistent, low-grade anger she could not shake. It appeared in small flashes—a sharp tone with her partner, a moment of irritation with her children. The anger felt untethered, and she worried it meant something was wrong with her.

As we stayed with it, the anger began to find its voice. It wasn't about her partner or her children at all. It was about the holidays themselves—the unspoken expectation that she would carry the emotional and logistical labor for everyone, and the reality that no one seemed to notice what it cost her.

The resentment had been carrying the cost in silence for years. It was the part of her that knew she was tired. The part that knew she was not, in fact, fine with doing it all. Her system had organized itself around being the capable one, the one who kept everything together. The resentment was the first crack in that identity.

Our values also shape what needs protecting. We instinctively protect what matters to us, and our values reveal what those things are. You may find yourself speaking up about something important, not because you are trying to create conflict, but because staying silent would feel like a form of self-abandonment. You may decline an invitation, not because you are exhausted, but because the event itself does not feel true to you.

This is not about rigidity or righteousness. It is simply the process of allowing your life to take shape around what is actually true, rather than around what keeps everything smooth.

What Protection Feels Like

For many people, the first experience of a boundary emerging from agency is not a firm "no." It is a pause.

Someone asks for something—your time, your energy, a change in plans—and instead of the reflexive "yes," there is a moment of hesitation. You might hear yourself say, "Let me think about it," or "I'll get back to you."

That pause is significant. It is the space between stimulus and response, the moment when the old pattern of automatic accommodation loosens. In that small pocket of time, you have the chance to check in with yourself and notice what is actually true.

Sometimes the answer will still be yes. Sometimes it will be no. The point is not the outcome. The point is the pause itself. The pause is the act of returning to yourself.

At other times, the expression of a boundary appears in different language. You might say, "I can't do that, but I can do this," or "I'm not available for that, but I appreciate you asking." The words are not aggressive or defensive. They are simply a statement of what is true in that moment.

Sometimes the expression of protection is physical distance. You might leave a room, end a conversation, or turn your body away. This is not necessarily a rejection of another person. It is simply the body moving toward a place that feels safer.

And sometimes protection appears as an apology. Not an apology for having the boundary itself, but an acknowledgment of impact. "I'm sorry I said that," or "I'm sorry I reacted that way." The apology does not undo the boundary. It recognizes the effect of what happened.

I once worked with a woman who was deeply afraid of disappointing people. She was a freelance designer and had developed a habit of saying yes to every project that came her way, even when she was already overloaded. She came to see me because she was burned out and resentful, yet she couldn't imagine saying no. The fear of disappointing someone felt bigger than the exhaustion she was carrying.

We began with the pause.

The next time a client asked for a rush project, she heard herself say, "Let me check my calendar and get back to you." For the next twenty-four hours, she lived in a quiet state of panic. Her mind generated every possible catastrophe. The client would be angry. She would lose the project. Her reputation would suffer.

But she didn't respond immediately. She let the pause hold.

When she finally looked at her calendar, the truth was obvious. She was completely booked. She wrote back and said, "I'm not going to be able to take this on right now, but I have an opening in two weeks."

The client replied, "Great. Let's book it."

What she said afterward stayed with me. "I realized I had been looking at my calendar for years," she said, "but I hadn't been feeling my calendar. I was treating my time like an infinite resource because I was so afraid of the word no."

The pause allowed her to feel the reality of her own limits.

When It Feels Hard

As these emotional signals begin to guide protection, capacity becomes what allows you to stay with the discomfort that sometimes follows. Capacity is the ability to remain with experience as it unfolds—both within yourself and in the presence of others.

It is not something you build. It is something that was always there, obscured for a long time by the fusion with protective patterns we encountered in Phase Two. As access to wholeness widens and the need to defend your existence loosens, that inherent capacity becomes available again.

Even when a boundary is received well, the internal experience can still be uncomfortable. The body may brace for consequences that never arrive. The old fear of abandonment may flicker. Guilt may surface.

The difference now is that those feelings no longer dictate your agency. They move through you like weather patterns moving across a sky that is wide enough to hold them.

What happens when someone reacts negatively to your boundary? When they push back, become angry, or try to evoke guilt? For many people, this is the deepest fear. For a long time, your system organized itself around preventing exactly this outcome. When it happens, it can feel like a catastrophic failure.

This is where capacity matters.

Capacity is the ability to feel another person's disappointment without making it a referendum on your worth. It is the ability to feel guilt without allowing it to drive your decisions. The work is not to eliminate the discomfort, but to remain present with it. In that presence, something becomes clear: you are larger than the feeling itself.

I once worked with a man who had long been the "good son" in his family. He was the one who never made waves, who showed up reliably, who cared for his aging parents without complaint. He loved them deeply, yet he was beginning to feel trapped by the role he had inhabited for decades.

One day, he decided to try something small. He told his parents he wouldn't be able to make his usual weekly visit because he needed the weekend to himself.

His mother reacted immediately.

"After all we've done for you," she said, disappointment sharp in her voice. "I guess we just won't see you then."

He described the moment as a physical blow. A wave of guilt rushed through him so intensely it made him nauseous. His first impulse was to take the boundary back, to apologize and promise he would come.

But he didn't.

"I'm sorry you're disappointed, Mom," he said. "I love you. I'll see you next week."

He spent the rest of the day in deep discomfort, convinced he had broken his mother's heart. Yet beneath the guilt he noticed something else—a solidity in his body. It was the feeling of not having abandoned himself.

He sat with both sensations, the guilt and the solidity, and allowed them to coexist. By the next day, the guilt had passed.

Pause and Notice: The Shape You Are In

Take a moment to notice the physical space your body is occupying. Feel the contact between your body and the chair, the floor, the ground beneath you. Notice the air against your skin. Without changing anything, simply arrive in the physical reality of your presence.

This is your starting point. This is the shape you are in right now.

Bring to mind a recent interaction—something simple, perhaps a brief conversation or a small moment of connection. As you recall it, notice what happens in your body. Do you feel a subtle leaning forward, an opening toward the other person? Or do you sense a slight pulling back, a tightening somewhere in your chest or shoulders?

There is no need to judge the response. Just notice it. This is the language of your boundaries.

Now think of a request someone made of you this week—a request for your time, your attention, or your energy. As you hold it in mind, notice what arises in your body. Is there a clear, uncomplicated yes? A solid no? Or something more complex—a flicker of resentment, a sense of obligation, a feeling of being stretched?

Stay with that sensation for a moment. It is telling you something about your capacity in that moment.

You do not need to act on this information right now. There is no immediate conversation to have or boundary to declare. Simply becoming familiar with the subtle language of your own presence is enough.

To feel the shape you are in, right here, right now.

The Direction You're Already Pointing

Human beings have a natural drive to orient. We are constantly, often without realizing it, organizing ourselves around what matters most. For much of our lives, this orienting happens unconsciously, guided by the need for safety, connection, and belonging. We learn to organize around the expectations of others, the rules of our culture, and the demands of survival. This is not a failure of awareness. It is the intelligence of a system learning how to move through the world.

When access to capacity begins to return, another layer of this orienting process becomes visible. The work of the previous sections—recognizing your needs and following the signals of your protection through boundaries—creates a subtle shift. You are no longer organized solely around what is required from the outside. A softer signal begins to register from within.

This is what I mean by values.

Values are not a set of moral rules to adopt or a list of qualities you are supposed to become. They are the expression of the human capacity to orient from the inside out. They are the felt sense of what matters most, the qualities of your own essential nature that give direction and coherence to your life. This section is not about constructing values. It is about learning to recognize the direction you are already pointing, and learning to live in alignment with it—even when doing so is difficult.

The Signals of Your Values

Values reveal themselves through response. The inner world is constantly registering what matters, and that registration shows up as feeling. It is not something you have to determine through analysis or arrive at through effort. It is already happening.

The question is not *What are my values?* but *Where are they already appearing?*

Resonance is one of the clearest signals. It appears as a sense of rightness—the satisfaction of doing something with care, the sense of being in the right place with the right people, the feeling that what you are doing belongs to you. These moments often seem ordinary, but they are not accidental. They are the nervous system registering contact with something meaningful. When something resonates, a value is present.

Anger and outrage carry the same intelligence. The things that ignite a fire in you—the injustices that make your chest tighten or your voice rise—point directly to what you care about. Anger is often treated as a problem to manage, but it is also a loyal signal. It appears most reliably at the edges of what you value, when something important to you is threatened or dismissed.

Envy and admiration are softer signals, but no less precise. When you find yourself drawn to a quality in another person—their courage, their freedom, their dedication to something meaningful—that pull is pointing somewhere inside you. What we admire in others often reflects a value we recognize but have not yet fully allowed into our own lives.

Guilt and shame are perhaps the most uncomfortable signals, but they can also be among the most faithful. Guilt arises when you sense that you have moved out of alignment with your own compass—when you said yes and meant no, when you stayed silent and wished you had spoken, when you turned away from something that mattered. Shame is the deeper version of this signal, the sense that you are not simply out of alignment but fundamentally wrong. Because shame often forms early and can become fused with identity, it is sometimes one of the hardest signals to interpret clearly. Yet even these painful emotions are orienting. They point back toward the direction your system is already trying to move.

I once worked with a man who had built a career that he was objectively very good at. He was respected, well-compensated, and successful by most external measures. Yet he described a persistent hollowness at the end of each day. He told me he didn't think of himself as someone who had strong values. Values, in his mind, belonged to people who were more certain than he was.

What we eventually discovered was that the hollowness itself was information. His life had been organized almost entirely around external markers of success, with very little contact with what actually mattered to him. When we began following the thread of what made him feel alive—a conversation that went somewhere real, the satisfaction of building something with his hands, the feeling of being genuinely useful to someone he cared about—a pattern began to appear.

The hollowness was not emptiness. It was the sound of his values going unheard.

The Direction You're Already Pointing

When we begin to listen to these signals—resonance, anger, admiration, guilt—something shifts in how we make decisions. We are no longer looking exclusively to the external world for direction. We begin consulting the internal compass that has been operating all along.

Values function as a compass in the lived sense. They are not abstract ideals but a felt reference point we can return to when a choice appears.

Listening to values rarely looks dramatic. It often appears in small, quiet moments. It is pausing before agreeing to something and noticing a subtle resistance. It is choosing a difficult conversation over an easier silence because something in you knows the silence will cost more. It is recognizing that the path that feels safe and the path that feels right are not the same—and choosing the one that feels right anyway.

The more often we respond to these signals rather than override them, the more trust begins to form. This is not trust as an idea. It is trust as an experience in the body. The nervous system learns that its signals are taken seriously. The system learns that it is safe to be heard.

Over time, this creates a positive loop. Listening builds trust. Trust increases access. Greater access makes listening easier.

I once worked with a woman who described this process as learning to take herself seriously. For most of her life, she had dismissed her own responses—overriding the flicker of resistance before agreeing to something, talking herself out of the pull toward what she actually wanted. Somewhere along the way, she had absorbed the belief that her inner responses were less reliable than the expectations of others.

As she began pausing long enough to notice what was happening inside her, something changed. Not suddenly, and not without difficulty. But she began to see that her responses were often accurate. The flicker of resistance was usually pointing toward something real. The pull toward something new was not random. The more she listened, the more she trusted. And the more she trusted, the easier it became to hear.

This is the ground of self-trust. Not the kind that comes from always making the right choice, but the kind that comes from knowing you remain in relationship with your own experience. You will not always be certain. You will not always move perfectly. But you are oriented. You know the direction you are already pointing, and you know how to find your way back when you drift.

Pause and Notice: Values As They Are Now

Bring your attention gently to your body and notice what is already present. Not what you believe should matter, but what actually carries weight.

You might recall a moment recently that felt clean and settled—a choice that landed without internal argument—or a moment that lingered with friction that seemed larger than the situation itself. Values often register in those places, through coherence or tension.

You may notice what consistently drains you even when it makes sense on paper, or what restores you without needing explanation. You may notice what you protect instinctively, what you grieve when it is missing, or what you admire in others without quite knowing why.

Stay close to how these experiences register physically. Perhaps there is a sense of ease, a tightening, clarity, or a subtle resistance. Values often speak through sensation before language.

You do not need to name them precisely. You do not need to decide what to do about them. Just notice where something feels aligned and where it does not.

Values do not need to be constructed. They are already shaping the way you move through the world. What matters here is not clarity but contact—remaining close enough to experience to recognize what carries weight as it appears.

Where We Become Known

To be human is to need connection. Our nervous systems are not self-contained; they exist in constant conversation with the nervous systems of others. This is why the idea of "self-work" can never be fully realized in isolation. The self does not exist in a vacuum. Our boundaries, our needs, our values—the very shape of who we are—become visible only in the presence of another.

For much of our lives, how we connect is not a conscious choice. It is an adaptation. We learn to organize ourselves around the needs and expectations of others in order to preserve the connection we depend on. Parts of ourselves that feel too risky, too much, or not enough are set aside so the relationship can continue. This is not a failure of character. It is the intelligence of a system that learned to survive.

But survival is not the same as aliveness. The emergence of agency and access to capacity—the ground cultivated in the previous phases—makes a different way of relating possible. Agency allows us to choose. Capacity allows us to remain present with ourselves even when connection feels uncertain or threatened. Together, they create the internal ground from which we can risk being seen as we are, rather than as we learned to be.

This is the shift from unconscious adaptation to agency. It is not a movement toward a perfect or frictionless state. It is the often awkward, imperfect, and necessary process of being human together. What follows is not a formula for harmony, but an exploration of what becomes possible when two people remain present in the shared space between them without abandoning themselves.

Being Human, Together

What does it look like to be in relationship from this place of emergent agency and capacity?

It does not look like perfection. It looks like the practice of staying. Staying with yourself. Staying with another. Staying in the awkwardness, the uncertainty, the unfinished space where something real is happening.

I think of a woman I worked with who had spent much of her life as the peacemaker in her family. During a tense dinner one evening, her sister made a passive-aggressive comment. The familiar sting arrived immediately, along with the conditioned urge to smooth everything over—to make a joke, redirect the conversation, manage her sister's mood.

In the past, she would have done exactly that, all while a knot of resentment tightened in her stomach. She would have abandoned her own hurt to maintain a false sense of peace.

This time, she did something different. She did nothing.

She felt the sting of the comment. She felt the urge to fix it. And she also felt her feet on the floor. She took a breath and stayed with the hurt long enough to recognize it as her own, without needing to extinguish it or redirect the moment. She did not lash out or withdraw. She simply allowed the comment to land.

The shift was almost entirely internal. She was no longer hostage to her sister's emotional state. She remained present inside her own experience, and from that place she could choose how—or whether—to respond.

Being human together can also look like a couple I once worked with who were trying to decide whether to move across the country. One partner felt energized by the idea, excited for a new chapter. The other felt deeply hesitant, full of fear about leaving their community behind.

Their old pattern was predictable. The excited partner would try to persuade and convince. The hesitant partner would shut down or agree reluctantly, planting the seeds of future resentment.

This time they tried something different. They stayed.

The excited partner shared their enthusiasm, but also made space for the other's experience. "I can see you're not feeling this the same way I am," they said. "What's coming up for you?"

Because that curiosity was genuine, the hesitant partner was able to speak from the fear rather than defend against it. "I'm scared of leaving our community," they said. "I'm worried I'll be lonely."

They were no longer standing on opposite sides of an argument. They were standing beside each other, looking at the same complexity from different vantage points. The conversation that followed was not about winning or persuading. It was about holding both realities at once—the excitement and the fear.

It was messy. There were tears. The outcome was uncertain.

But for the first time, they were in the decision together.

This is the texture of a relationship in which two people have enough ground in themselves to truly meet each other. It is slow, often unglamorous work, but it is also profoundly moving. It is the experience of being human together.

Pause and Notice: Relating from Agency

Bring to mind a relationship that carries weight in your life. It does not need to be the most important or the most difficult. Just one that is present.

Notice how your system organizes itself around this person. Is there a sense of ease, a feeling that you can rest in their presence? Or is there a subtle, ongoing effort—a sense that you need to be a particular version of yourself in order to maintain the connection?

Think of a recent interaction between the two of you. As you recall it, notice what happens in your body. Do you feel a slight leaning forward, an opening toward the other person? Or is there a tightening, a pull to manage or withdraw?

This is the nonverbal language of the relationship.

What do you tend to sacrifice when disconnection feels possible in this relationship? Your values? Your time? Your energy? What does it cost you to keep the connection intact?

Now imagine remaining in contact with yourself while still staying in relationship—even if the relationship changes shape.

You do not need an answer right now. Just stay with the question.

Rupture and Repair: The Rhythm of Connection

It is a myth that healthy relationships are free of conflict. Connection is not forged in the absence of disconnection but in the willingness to repair it.

Relationship is not a steady state. It is a rhythm—a continual movement between rupture and repair. Within that rhythm, we come to know each other more fully.

A rupture is any moment when the connection breaks. It may be a sharp word, a missed moment of attention, or a misunderstanding that leaves a lingering sting. In those moments, our conditioning moves quickly to the surface. Protective patterns activate. Old strategies—attack, withdrawal, explanation, blame—appear almost instantly. This is not evidence that the relationship is failing. It is evidence that vulnerable parts of us are trying to protect themselves.

In a rupture, our protective selves become visible.

Access to capacity changes what becomes possible next. Immediately after a rupture, access to our wider self often narrows. The reaction is quick and protective. But capacity allows us to tolerate the intensity of that narrowing long enough to recognize what is happening.

Instead of reacting immediately, we pause. The nervous system begins to widen again. From that wider place, we can see our own reaction without being consumed by it.

Shame or hurt may still be present, but they no longer define the moment.

It is from this wider ground that repair becomes possible.

Repair is the conscious decision to turn back toward the relationship after the break. It is the space where our vulnerable insides have a chance to be seen. Because we can stay with our own experience, we can risk sharing it. We can tolerate the possibility that the repair may not be met perfectly—or even met at all—without losing ourselves in the process.

I think of a woman who once described an argument with her partner. In the middle of the conflict, she said something sharp and dismissive. The rupture was immediate. Her partner's face fell, and he left the room. In the past, she would have been swept into a storm of shame that quickly hardened into defensiveness. She would have followed him not to repair but to argue—to explain why his reaction was unfair.

This time, she stayed where she was.

She felt the shame—hot, familiar, insistent. She felt the fear that she had ruined everything. But she also had enough capacity to remain present with it. She recognized the pattern: when she feels exposed, she attacks. After a few minutes, she went to her partner.

Instead of defending herself, she said, "What I said was sharp and unkind. When you questioned my decision, I felt a wave of panic, and I lashed out. That's my pattern. It wasn't okay, and I can see how much it hurt you."

Her partner felt the shift immediately. Because she was not defending or attacking, he did not need to armor himself in return.

"It did hurt," he said. "It made me feel like my opinion doesn't matter to you."

They were no longer opponents. They were standing together, looking at the same wound.

Repair does not erase rupture. It transforms it. Each time this cycle is navigated consciously, another layer is added to the story of the relationship. The story becomes less about perfection and more about resilience. We begin to trust that connection can hold the truth of our reactive, protective parts—and still hold us.

Pause and Notice: The Space Between

Bring to mind a recent conversation. As you recall it, notice what happens in your body. Is there ease, a sense of openness? Or is there a subtle bracing, a feeling of being on guard?

Now think of someone you feel close to. As you imagine them, what is the first sensation that arises in your body? Warmth? Tension? Expansion? Contraction?

This is the nonverbal language of relationship.

Recall a recent moment of disagreement or misunderstanding. Notice the impulse that appears in your body. Do you feel the urge to fix the situation immediately, to explain, to apologize? Or do you feel a pull to withdraw and create distance?

Is there space to remain present with the discomfort for even a moment longer?

You do not need to do anything with what you notice. For now, simply observe the landscape of your connections. Feel the space between you and another person, and notice what happens within that space.

When Agency Wavers

There may be weeks when things feel clear. You notice your needs before depletion arrives. You say no without rehearsing it. You move through your days with a steadiness that does not feel manufactured. It is not euphoric. It is simply ordinary—and because it feels ordinary, you trust it.

Then life shifts. Your child becomes sick. Work compresses into fewer hours. Your sleep is broken. And the old organization returns.

You hear yourself agreeing too quickly. You find yourself smoothing, explaining, and orienting toward others before locating yourself. The first feeling that appears is often disappointment. The familiar thought follows quickly: *How did it disappear so fast?*

This is not a reversal. It is the nervous system responding to conditions.

When the system is under pressure—fatigue, conflict, uncertainty—it narrows its focus to manage the demand. It has not betrayed you. It is doing exactly what it learned to do to survive.

The shift comes when you stop treating the return of old patterns as proof that the alignment was false.

I once worked with a woman who noticed her jaw clenched and her thoughts racing during a rushed morning. In the past, she would have interpreted this as failure, a sign that she had returned to the beginning.

This time, she simply registered what was happening.

"I'm braced," she said.

That recognition was the return—not a return to calm, but a return to contact with her experience. As the pressure of the week passed, her sense of steadiness returned without being forced.

Agency and capacity are not states you maintain. They are places you return to.

The invitation of this phase is not to eliminate wavering but to change your relationship to it—to recognize the tightening when it appears and meet it without judgment. In this way, wavering becomes part of the unfolding rather than evidence against it.

Living Emerging

You may notice yourself speaking more directly in conversation. You pause before reacting. You feel what you want or need with less internal negotiation.

These moments do not appear consistently. They arise alongside familiar patterns, sometimes briefly, sometimes unexpectedly. The roles and protections that formed earlier in life do not disappear. What changes is how much they organize your experience.

In relationships, you may find yourself staying present during a difficult conversation rather than leaving internally. You may notice a boundary sooner, or recognize that something feels off without immediately overriding that awareness.

Sometimes you will still accommodate or withdraw. Sometimes you will not.

There may also be moments of increased aliveness. Curiosity may return in small ways. Interests that were dormant for years may resurface. At the same time, vulnerability often becomes more visible. When identity no longer organizes experience as tightly, emotions can feel closer to the surface.

This can feel unfamiliar, even unsettling, especially if you have long relied on control or distance to hold yourself together. Nothing has gone wrong when this happens. Your capacity is reorganizing alongside your responsiveness.

For a long time, agency may have felt like work—something to assert, defend, or perform. As the effort of holding yourself together loosens, agency becomes something different. It is no longer something you generate. It is something you return to.

Choice begins to feel less like calculation and more like recognition. Action arises not because it should, but because it is the most natural expression of what is already true.

This is where self-trust begins to grow. Not certainty about outcomes, but trust in your own perception—trust that what you feel is real, that what you need matters, that your sense of direction is worth following.

For a long time, that trust may have been buried beneath the effort of managing yourself into a different shape. When that effort softens, something becomes clear: you were always a reliable witness to your own experience.

What is emerging was never absent.

It is simply becoming easier to access.

Chapter 16

The Phase of Animating

Aliveness is the starting point. It is the simple, biological fact of being a living body in a living world. It is the breath moving in your chest, the heart beating in your ribs, the nervous system adjusting to the light and the sound and the temperature of the room you are in right now. You are not doing any of this. It is what it means to be alive.

For a long time, you may have lived at a distance from this. A nervous system that learned, under certain conditions, that managing life was safer than living it. That standing apart from experience was the price of surviving it. You learned to watch yourself from the inside, to evaluate, adjust, and override the signals your body was sending, to stay one step ahead of whatever might happen next. This was the intelligence of a system doing exactly what it was designed to do.

But it came at a cost. The persistent sense of being outside of your own existence. Of watching life happen, not inside it. Of knowing, somewhere beneath the management, that something was being missed.

Phase Four is about recognizing what was never gone.

The animating life—the body's natural, pre-conscious capacity to respond, to reach, to rest, to withdraw, to engage—was always here. It was held at a distance by the effort of protection. As the strategies of the earlier phases soften, what returns is the original, biological fact of being a living body in a living world. The breath deepens on its own. The body moves toward what it needs without being instructed. Life begins to happen through you, not managed by you.

This is what we call animation. And it is something you allow yourself to return to.

Everything needed is already here. It always was.

This phase shows up in small ways that are easy to miss if you are looking for something big.

It is the moment you realize you have been standing at the window for five minutes, not thinking about anything, just watching the light change. And instead of snapping back to productivity, you stay there a little longer.

It is noticing you are hungry and eating something—because your body asked for it and you listened.

It is being in a conversation, feeling the urge to change the subject, and changing it. Without apologizing. Without explaining why.

It is getting into bed earlier than planned because you are tired, even though there are still things on your list. Because your body is done, and you are letting that be enough.

Animation is ordinary. It is life happening through, and most of the time it just feels like living.

Animating Life

Life is already moving. Before attention settles anywhere, something is happening. Breath shifts. Muscles engage or release. A pull toward movement arises, or a need to pause registers. Energy gathers, disperses, wanes. The body is already participating.

This animating life is subtle. It shows up as a lean forward, a hesitation, a deepening of breath, a turning away, a need for rest, a desire to speak, or the impulse to remain silent. These are the body orienting itself moment by moment within changing conditions. They are life expressing itself through you before you have had a chance to intervene.

For most of your life, you may have noticed these signals and acted on them immediately. Felt the hesitation and pushed through it. Felt the need for rest and overrode it. Felt the impulse to speak and swallowed it. This is what management looks like from the inside: a constant interruption of the body's natural movement. The habituated response of a system that learned, long ago, that its own signals were less reliable than the demands of the environment.

I worked with someone who said she noticed this for the first time during a phone call with her sister. They were talking about logistics, but halfway through the conversation, she felt her jaw tighten, and her shoulders pull up toward her ears. She had not been aware of doing it. It was simply happening.

In the past, she would have either ignored it entirely or tried to fix it—rolling her shoulders, forcing herself to relax. This time, she just noticed it. The tightness was there. Her body was responding to something, though she could not name what. Maybe the tone of her sister's voice. Maybe the pace of the conversation. Maybe just the accumulated tension of the day.

She did not try to make it go away. She stayed on the phone, aware of the tightness, and kept talking. A few minutes later, without her doing anything, her jaw released slightly. Her breath deepened on its own. The tightness was still there, but it had shifted. Life was moving through her body, adjusting and responding without her needing to direct it.

This is what becomes possible when the interruption softens. The ordinary experience of the body doing what it was always designed to do: responding to life as it is actually happening, rather than as it has been managed to appear.

You only need to stop interrupting it.

Pause and Notice: Inhabiting Aliveness

Here, attention turns toward what is already being lived.

The body is already in contact with the surface beneath it. Weight distributes. Muscles engage or release. Some areas settle while others hold. There may be ease, resistance, restlessness, or very little sensation at all. Each of these reflects how life is organizing itself in this moment.

Sensation arrives in its own order. Sometimes it is clear and specific. At other times, it is diffuse, faint, or barely noticeable. Warmth, pressure, tingling, heaviness, distance—any of these may be present, or none of them distinctly so. The body remains responsive even without vivid sensation.

Attention moves as it moves. It may linger somewhere, gather briefly, drift, or lose its place entirely. This movement is part of how experience unfolds.

Breath is already moving. Its rhythm shifts without instruction. The body adjusts around it, responding to internal and external conditions without needing guidance.

Numbness, distance, or restlessness are also expressions of how the system is responding right now. They are not interruptions.

I once sat with someone who talked about lying on the floor one afternoon—not because she had decided to practice embodiment or do a body scan, but because she was exhausted and the floor was closer than the couch. She lay there staring at the ceiling, feeling nothing in particular.

She described it as flat. No strong sensations. No emotional clarity. Just a dull, distant kind of presence. In earlier years, she would have interpreted this as dissociation, as evidence that she was disconnected or shut down. She would have tried to get back into her body through breathing exercises or movement.

This time, she just stayed there—flat, distant, and not particularly alive-feeling. After a while—she could not say how long—she noticed a small shift. A slight heaviness in her legs. A coolness on the back of her neck where it touched the floor. Small, subtle sensations that were there once she stopped trying to make anything happen.

The flatness did not disappear, but it was no longer the only thing present. Her body was still responding, still alive, even when it did not feel vibrant or engaged.

Animation is sometimes nothing more than the fact of being here.

Letting Life Lead

Letting life lead means staying with what is happening without trying to direct it. The body is already responding, already adjusting, already participating in the world. Your role is simply to stop getting in the way.

This is a subtle shift. It is the difference between noticing you are tired and deciding to rest, and resting because you are tired. The first is an act of management. The second is participation. In the first, you remain in charge; in the second, you allow yourself to be part of the flow.

I worked with a woman who described a moment in her kitchen. She was making dinner, moving through familiar steps, when she felt a wave of exhaustion. Her first impulse was to push through and finish what she had started. Her second thought was to practice self-care—to give herself permission to rest. Both were forms of management.

This time she did neither. She simply stopped. Leaning against the counter, she closed her eyes. She did not decide to rest. She just rested. She did not reassure herself that it was okay. She allowed the moment to be exactly what it was. After a few minutes, the exhaustion passed, and she returned to making dinner.

Nothing had been solved or fixed. But for a moment, she had let life lead.

To let life lead is to trust that the body knows what it is doing. That it knows when to move and when to be still, when to speak and when to remain silent, when to engage and when to withdraw. The shift is not learning a new technique. It is recognizing that the intelligence organizing life was already here.

Pause and Notice: Letting Life Lead

Here, attention rests on the movement of life itself.

Notice the rhythm of your breath. The rise and fall of your chest. The way the air moves in and out of your body. You are not doing this. It is happening.

Notice the sensations in your body—warmth, coolness, pressure, tingling. You are not creating these sensations. They are arising.

Notice the sounds in the room: the hum of the refrigerator, distant traffic, the sound of your own breathing. You are not producing these sounds. They are simply present.

Notice the thoughts that come and go—plans, memories, worries, daydreams. You are not authoring these thoughts. They appear, move through, and pass.

Life is happening. You are not in charge of it. You are part of it.

I worked with someone who described realizing she was tired halfway through a meeting she had already agreed to attend. Not the dramatic kind of tired that demands attention, but a dull thinning—words landing a little later, posture beginning to collapse, the familiar urge to push through. In the past, she would have stayed until the end, collected herself afterward, and told herself it didn't matter.

What was different was not a decision to honor her body. It was the moment she noticed her attention drifting toward the door and didn't pull it back. She allowed the impulse to leave to register without turning it into justification. When a natural pause came, she simply said she needed to step out and did.

The movement was small. No one reacted. Nothing was resolved.

Later, she noticed there was no crash afterward—no resentment, no story about weakness or inconsideration. Just the sense that something had completed when it needed to. The body had led, and she had followed without taking over.

This does not mean access remains constant. Under pressure, habits of control may return. Attention may move ahead of experience, and response may become hurried or rigid. When this happens, nothing has failed. Life has reorganized around protection again.

Leadership returns as soon as participation becomes available, without correction.

Letting life lead is remaining with yourself as experience moves. From that place, action carries less force, restraint carries less tension, and choice emerges without being demanded. Life leads because it is already in motion.

Another client described a moment in the middle of an argument with her partner. They had been circling the same issue for twenty minutes, voices raised, both frustrated. She could feel herself gearing up for another round—preparing her next point, gathering evidence, ready to defend her position.

Then something stopped her. Not a conscious decision. Not a thought like *I should take a break*. Just a sudden absence of energy for continuing. The fight was still there. Her partner was still talking. But something in her had gone quiet.

She said, "I need to stop."

Not *let's take a break* or *can we talk about this later*. Just: *I need to stop*.

Her partner looked surprised but nodded. She walked into the other room and sat on the edge of the bed.

She didn't know if she had done the right thing. She didn't feel resolved or relieved. She simply knew she couldn't keep going, and for the first time, she allowed that knowing to lead rather than override it.

The argument wasn't resolved that night. Something else had happened—she had followed life instead of forcing it.

Inhabiting Aliveness

Inhabiting aliveness feels like a fit. Something aligns. A moment settles. A choice lands without needing justification. Often, you recognize it only afterward, because there was no internal friction while it was happening.

It appears in small ways. You pause instead of pushing through. You speak and then stop, sensing that what needed to be said has already been said. You rest without negotiating with yourself. You take a different route home because your body slows at the thought of the usual one.

These movements are not calculated. They arise from contact and carry their own sense of rightness, even when they remain incomplete or provisional.

Living this way produces a different kind of consistency. Some days are open and responsive. Others are dense, quiet, or constrained. Aliveness expresses itself differently depending on energy, demand, and context. What remains steady is the relationship to the feeling, not the feeling itself.

You stay with what is present without elevating it, resolving it, or turning it into something else. Experience is allowed to be exactly as it is, including when it is unremarkable.

Animation becomes visible in how you move through ordinary life. In how you walk when there is no urgency. In how you rest without earning it. In how you engage when something opens, and withdraw when it closes. In how you stop performing for outcome and begin responding to what is actually here. You sense these movements and follow them.

Time feels different here. Decisions are not rushed because listening has replaced urgency. There is more space between impulse and action, created through presence. Even doing very little can feel active when it comes from contact rather than avoidance.

Difficulty is carried differently as well. Fatigue registers as information rather than resistance. Tension can exist without immediate correction. Pleasure can be noticed without grasping at it.

Aliveness includes all of this. It is defined by participation.

Pause and Notice: Listening to Aliveness

Sometimes a subtle impulse appears—a leaning, a shift, a desire to change position. It does not insist on being followed. It registers.

If nothing calls for movement, nothing is required. Stillness is already a form of responsiveness.

When an impulse does appear, it is often small. A shoulder rolls. Weight shifts. The spine adjusts. You stand, or you settle more fully into where you are. These movements are life responding to itself.

What matters here is that the movement is allowed. Sensation moves. The body reorganizes. Something completes without being evaluated or explained.

Afterward, life continues. The body may feel different. It may feel the same. The movement was not made to improve experience, only to follow what was already emerging.

This is how animation becomes lived. Life moves in small, ordinary ways when it is given room.

This way of inhabiting life feels less like something you are practicing and more like something you recognize. You are no longer standing outside of what is already happening. Life is lived from the inside, through a body that adjusts, responds, and rests as conditions change.

Nothing here resolves uncertainty or simplifies complexity. Experience is carried without interruption. From this place, what has emerged does not need to be protected or enforced. It is lived, moment by moment, as life continues to move.

When Aliveness Pulls Back

Aliveness does not move in a straight line. There are times when energy recedes, movement quiets, and engagement becomes more contained. This, too, is part of how life moves. Expansion and contraction both allow experience to remain viable across changing conditions.

When aliveness pulls back, the body conserves. Sensation may feel muted or distant. Interest softens. Participation becomes more reserved or more selective. These shifts often arise in response to fatigue, loss, sustained demand, or intensity that has exceeded what feels manageable. Life adjusts in order to continue.

For many people, these moments are uncomfortable. There can be an impulse to restore momentum, to return to a familiar sense of vitality, or to interpret the quiet as a sign that something has gone wrong. That urgency often reflects earlier conditions where pulling back carried risk—where withdrawal threatened connection, usefulness, or belonging. In those contexts, staying alive required staying available even when capacity was limited.

Within this phase, contraction is met differently. It is recognized as responsiveness rather than regression. Aliveness has reorganized. What is needed here is allowance—room for life to move more quietly without being pressured to reappear.

Allowing aliveness to pull back does not mean passivity. It means remaining present without forcing movement. Rest is permitted to be rest. Stillness is allowed to last. The absence of momentum is not treated as a problem to solve. When contraction can exist without urgency, the need for protection through collapse or control softens, because withdrawal no longer carries the same threat.

I worked with someone who spoke about a stretch of weeks where nothing seemed to move. She wasn't exactly distressed, but her energy stayed low. Invitations felt heavy. Even things she usually enjoyed registered as distant. Her first instinct was to assume something was wrong—that she was withdrawing, avoiding, slipping backward.

Over time, she noticed that the inward pull had a rhythm. She slept more, chose simpler food, and allowed conversations to end sooner without trying to repair them. There was no drama in it, only a steady quieting. When she stopped trying to interpret the contraction, she felt how precise it was—how much effort it would have taken to push herself back into momentum.

Eventually, without decision, interest returned. She reached out to one person, took a longer walk, and stayed engaged a little longer than before. Nothing had been solved. The inward movement had simply finished what it needed to finish. Aliveness had not disappeared. It had been conserving itself.

Movement returns on its own. Energy gathers. Interest stirs. Engagement becomes possible again. This return does not happen because it was summoned, but because the conditions for participation have shifted. Life resumes when it is ready.

Remaining with contraction without abandoning yourself deepens trust in the rhythm of experience. Aliveness begins to be recognized in quiet as well as in expression, in retreat as well as in reach. Neither needs to be defended against. Both are part of how life maintains continuity across time.

When aliveness pulls back, nothing essential has been lost. The current has slowed. Staying with that slowing—without judgment, urgency, or interpretation—allows animation to remain intact, even in its quieter forms.

Responding From Relationship

There are moments when staying present does not hold everything on its own. Experience registers in the body and signals when something needs to change. Animation includes action that emerges from contact rather than urgency.

At times, this begins with a sense that something is strained or misaligned—physical discomfort, emotional pressure, mental fatigue, or a subtle feeling of being overwhelmed. The response does not need to come from habit or from the demand to fix what is happening. It can arise from recognition alone.

An impulse may appear. It may feel vague at first, more like a leaning than a clear direction. Staying with it allows it to take shape on its own. What initially registers as "something needs to change" often turns out to be something more specific. What is needed may not be resolution, but adjustment.

The body may signal a shift in position, a step away, a pause, or a hand placed somewhere supportive. It may move toward slowing down or toward engagement. It may ask for space, warmth, water, movement, or for an interaction to end sooner than planned. These responses arise as part of participation.

When a response becomes available, it can be followed without aiming for relief or improvement. Action here is not meant to optimize experience, but to remain in relationship with it.

Afterward, experience continues. Urgency may lessen or remain. Sensation may change or stay the same. What matters is not the outcome, but whether contact was maintained through the response. This is what participation looks like in this phase. Experience is neither controlled nor abandoned. You stay close enough to respond without taking over.

Someone I worked with once described being at home mid-morning, halfway through a familiar routine. Nothing felt particularly wrong, yet her body kept hesitating—hands slowing, attention drifting, a subtle resistance to continuing. In the past, she would have pushed through, finished what she started, and dealt with the exhaustion later. This time, she noticed the hesitation without correcting it.

She found herself sitting down instead. Not as a decision and not with relief—just a simple shift. A few minutes passed. Her breath changed slightly. Some of the tightness remained. When she stood again, she did not return to the task. She sent a short message canceling something scheduled for later that afternoon. The words came without rehearsal.

Nothing was clarified afterward. No sense of having made the right choice arrived. The day did not feel better or worse, only different—less directed, less organized around momentum. What mattered was that the hesitation had been allowed to interrupt the routine without explanation or justification. The movement had been lived, even without a conclusion.

Aliveness is Shared

As animation becomes more familiar, experience no longer feels confined to an interior space. You do not sense life as something happening inside you and then expressed outward into relationship. You feel it as already moving through contact—shaped by proximity, response, timing, and presence that do not belong to one body alone.

Aliveness is relational by nature. The body responds not only to its own rhythms, but to tone, pacing, and the subtle shifts that occur between people. Attention adjusts to what is happening in shared space. Breath slows when another settles nearby. Posture softens when you meet tension rather than resist it. Energy steadies when you receive presence. These movements may be quiet and easily missed, yet they are how experience organizes itself moment to moment.

It may also become clear that this responsiveness is not limited to human interaction. The body adjusts to light, temperature, sound, and environment without instruction. Pace changes with seasons, fatigue, and demand. Attention sharpens or softens in response to space, silence, crowding, or openness. Aliveness is continuously shaped by conditions that extend beyond any single relationship or individual life—contexts present long before any person arrived and that will continue after they are gone.

Life, as it is felt here, is the animating movement it-self—the capacity for response, adjustment, and contact that moves through bodies, relationships, and conditions. The human condition is how life is lived: within time, limitation, vulnerability, meaning-making, and relationship. Aliveness does not resolve these constraints. It moves through them.

Wholeness, in this sense, is not something private that you must maintain through effort or self-sufficiency. You do not generate it internally and then carry it into relationship. It is something you are held within, together.

Someone once described sitting across from a close friend at the end of a long day. Neither of them was talking much. The conversation had thinned out on its own, leaving long pauses neither rushed to fill. At one point, the friend exhaled and leaned back in her chair. Without intending to, she felt her shoulders drop, and her breath deepen in response. Nothing had been said. Nothing needed to be.

Later, she realized that something had settled between them, a shared easing. She hadn't been monitoring herself or tracking the interaction. Her body had responded before she thought to notice it. The moment passed as quietly as it arrived. What stayed with her was the sense that connection had happened without effort, as if life itself had moved through the space they were sharing and then continued on.

For many people, this recognition comes in moments when conversation does not require vigilance, when you can tolerate difference without managing the exchange, or when the effort to stay intact eases because connection no longer feels precarious. Wholeness becomes less about containment and more about being held within a larger movement of experience.

This does not mean that relationships become seamless or free of impact. Misattunement still occurs. Distance still arises. Disappointment remains part of shared life. What shifts is the assumption that these moments threaten integrity or require self-abandonment to endure. The body no longer organizes as if rupture equals collapse, or as if you must preserve connection at the cost of internal access.

As you trust animation, the need to brace against relationship softens. You can hold boundaries without hardening. Presence can remain even when outcomes are uncertain. Repair becomes possible without urgency. You preserve integrity not through control, but through staying in contact with what is real—both internally and between bodies.

Phase Four reveals that aliveness was never an individual possession. It has always been shared—shaped through interaction, sustained through contact, and carried by conditions larger than any single life. What once felt fragile or conditional appears as more durable, not because you defend it, but because you do not carry it alone. Animation does not draw life inward. It returns experience to participation. The body lives its life in constant relationship with the world around it. Aliveness does not end at the boundary of the self. It moves through it—shared, responsive, and ongoing.

Pause and Notice: Aliveness in Contact

Recall a recent moment of being with another person—a conversation, shared task, brief exchange, or quiet presence.

Without analyzing the interaction, notice what was happening between you.

A shift in tone. A pause that changed the rhythm. A softening, tightening, or settling that did not belong to either of you alone.

What did your body register in response to that shared moment?

Notice whether anything changed through being met—not resolved, not improved, just received. What matters is not the outcome of the interaction, but the fact that experience did not need to be carried alone.

Someone I worked with once told me about sitting with her young daughter, who was upset about something at school. Her daughter was crying, not obviously, just steady tears and halting words. The client's instinct was to fix it—to offer solutions, to reassure, to make the crying stop.

She noticed something. Every time she started to speak, to offer comfort or advice, her daughter's body would tense slightly. The crying would get louder or more jagged. When she stopped talking and just sat close, her daughter's breath would even out a little. The tears would still come, but more smoothly.

So she stopped trying to help. She just sat there, one hand on her daughter's back, breathing steadily. She wasn't trying to regulate her daughter. She was just present. And, without anyone doing anything, her daughter's crying began to slow. Her breath shifted, matching her mother's rhythm. The upset was still there, but it was being held differently.

Later, her daughter said, "Thanks for not trying to make me feel better." It was the first time the client realized that her presence—just her steady, non-anxious presence—was doing something her words never could. Aliveness wasn't something she was offering her daughter. It was something moving between them, shared and responsive, without either of them having to make it happen.

Meaning as Recognition

Earlier in this process, meaning functioned as a filter. It was shaped by conditioning—by what you learned to believe about yourself, what you were taught to want, and what you came to expect from life. Experience arrived and was immediately sorted: significant or insignificant, progress or failure, proof of something or evidence of something else. Meaning was not something you chose. It was the lens through which everything passed.

From here, that lens begins to clear.

Meaning does not have to be constructed. It does not need to be earned, assembled, or justified. Meaning is already present in the fact of being alive—in the breath moving through the body, in the conversation that lands, in the ordinary Tuesday that asks nothing of you and offers itself anyway. It appears not as significance you must locate, but as the texture of experience itself.

This is what aliveness reveals: meaning was never something you had to become worthy of. It was always here, woven into the ordinary.

Freed from the filter, meaning is no longer a verdict on how well you are living. It is no longer evidence of progress or proof of growth. It does not require suffering to justify it or achievement to validate it. It is not located only in the moments that stand out—the breakthroughs, the clarity, the times you showed up exactly as you hoped you would. It is present in all of it: in the difficult seasons and the unremarkable ones, in the moments of contact and the moments of distance, in the life you are already living.

The pressure to make something of your life—to grow enough, understand enough, arrive somewhere—was the filter talking. Without it, what remains is simpler.

You are alive. That is already something.

I worked with someone who had spent years trying to build a life that felt meaningful. She had done the work—the therapy, the reflection, the careful choices. And still something felt thin, as if she were always one step away from the life that would finally count.

One afternoon, she was folding laundry while her daughter sat nearby on the floor, talking about nothing in particular. A show she had watched. A friend at school. The client was only half listening, thinking about everything she still needed to do.

And then she stopped.

She looked at her daughter. She felt the warm weight of the folded shirt in her hands. She heard her daughter's voice—the particular rhythm of it, the way she paused before the funny part of a story.

Nothing unusual was happening. Yet it was enough. More than enough. It was full.

She told me later that she had spent so long trying to locate meaning that she had missed it being everywhere. It was not in the accomplishments or the breakthroughs. It was in the laundry, her daughter's voice, and the ordinary afternoon that had asked nothing of her and given her everything.

This is what meaning looks like when the filter loosens. It does not arrive as insight or reward.

It was already here. It has always been here.

Living Animating

The changes are subtle. You notice you are speaking more directly. You pause instead of reacting. You sense what you want or need with less internal negotiation. These moments appear alongside familiar patterns, sometimes unexpectedly and sometimes briefly. Identity does not disappear. What changes is how much it organizes your experience.

This is what it feels like to be in relationship with participation, freed from the need to control it. For a long time, participation was conditional. It depended on feeling a certain way—engaged, energized, inspired. We tried to manufacture aliveness, managing our experience so it would match our idea of what a good life should be. When that control loosens, you are free to be in your life as it is.

You are not trying to make it anything. You are simply in it. The texture of ordinary moments becomes enough. You taste the food. The conversation lands. The quiet afternoon is just a quiet afternoon, and that is not a problem. You are no longer waiting for life to begin. You are already in it.

Energy begins to move differently in the body. Curiosity returns. Interests that were dormant for a long time surface again as the effort of holding yourself together loosens. At the same time, vulnerability often becomes more visible. When identity organizes experience less tightly, emotions sit closer to the surface. Your sensitivity may increase before your stability does.

This can feel unfamiliar or even unsettling, especially if you are used to holding yourself together through control or distance. Nothing is going wrong. Your capacity is reorganizing alongside your responsiveness.

In relationships, contact begins to happen differently. You stay present during a difficult conversation rather than mentally check out. You sense a boundary sooner. You recognize when something feels wrong without immediately overriding that awareness. At times, you will still accommodate or withdraw. At other times, you will not. The system gradually learns that it can remain intact without protecting itself as fiercely as it once did.

What is emerging was never absent. It is simply becoming easier to access.

Chapter 17

The Phase of Returning

This phase has a texture I recognize. It is the feeling after a hard week where I felt completely lost, and then one morning, I woke up, and the familiar weight on my chest was lighter. Nothing has changed, but something has settled.

It is noticing an old pattern of anxiety arise, and instead of the usual panic or the effort to fix it, there is recognition: Oh, this again. The reaction to the reaction is different. Less struggle. More space.

It is having a difficult conversation and realizing, only after it is over, that you stayed. You were present, even in the discomfort. You did not disappear. You did not perform. You were just there.

This phase is about the return. It is about the growing trust that even when you lose contact with yourself, you come back — and that the coming back happens on its own, when the conditions are right.

Returning is the recognition that you were never truly gone. You were just oriented somewhere else for a little while.

By this point in the process, you are no longer learning something new. You are not being handed another framework or asked to hold yourself differently. The work has shifted. It is less about understanding and more about staying — staying in relationship with yourself as life keeps moving, as conditions change, as familiar things return.

And they do return. That is the thing no one tells you. You do the work, and then life keeps happening. The difficult relationship does not resolve. The anxiety comes back. The old pattern surfaces in a new situation. You find yourself, again, in familiar terrain.

This is not failure. This is the human condition.

Access comes and goes. There are days when you feel close to yourself — when the body is familiar, when something true registers without effort, when you move through the world with a kind of ease you have worked hard to find. And there are days when attention tightens, old responses take over, and experience organizes itself around urgency or distance or a story you thought you were done telling.

What you have learned does not disappear in those moments. It becomes less visible. It lives in the fact that you no longer interpret the contraction as proof of something, that you can stay with uncertainty a little longer before forcing it into an explanation, that the relationship with yourself continues even when access feels thin.

You were never moving toward a version of yourself untouched by life. You were learning to stay in contact even as life affected you. That contact looks like presence when it is available. It looks like allowance when it is not. The process continues here — gradually, imperfectly, and wholly intact.

Returning Without Making Meaning

Experience does not move in a straight line. Familiar patterns reappear. Old responses return. Ways of organizing that once felt resolved surface again under new conditions. This is what it means to live inside time, relationship, and change.

What arrives first is often the meaning — before the experience itself has even settled. Contraction becomes evidence. The hard week becomes a verdict. The old pattern becomes proof that nothing has actually changed, that you have lost ground, that the work was not real.

Someone I worked with described a week where everything felt hard. Small tasks took longer. Conversations required more energy. She found herself snapping at her kids over things that normally would not have bothered her. By the end of the week, she was exhausted and frustrated with herself.

The old version of her would have spiraled: I've regressed. I'm not doing the work. I've lost my progress. Something is wrong with me. She would have tried to figure out what she had done wrong and how to get back to where she had been.

This time, she noticed something simpler. This week is hard. I'm more reactive. I'm tired. And she let that be enough. She did not try to fix it or understand it. She just lived through it.

The following week, things eased. Not because she had done anything, but because conditions had shifted. Her kids were less demanding. Work was lighter. She had slept more. The reactivity faded. She had made it through a hard week without letting it become a verdict about who she was.

This is what changes. Not the hard weeks. Not the old patterns. Not the fact that life keeps arriving with its full weight. What changes is how much you need to make of it.

When Nothing Seems to Be Happening

There are stretches in this process where nothing seems to be happening. The language that once felt close no longer resonates. The familiar sense of contact softens. Experience feels ordinary, muted, and attention turns outward toward the simple demands of living — the job, the kids, the logistics, the next thing.

This is not stagnation. This is integration.

Change continues during these stretches. It just does not arrive. What shifts does not always arrive with clarity or emotional movement. Some things settle so quietly that you only notice them later, when you realize that something which once required effort is no longer effortful. What once needed to be tracked has become the way you move.

Someone I worked with described a six-month period when she barely thought about any of this work. She was not avoiding it. She was not resisting it. It just was not present. Her life was full — a new job, a move, her daughter starting school. She was busy, engaged, living.

Occasionally she would have a passing thought: I haven't been paying attention to my body. I haven't been noticing my patterns. But the thought would come and go without sticking. She did not feel guilty. She did not feel like she was failing. It just was not where her attention was.

Then one day, months later, she was in a meeting that would have normally sent her into anxiety. High stakes, people she wanted to impress, the potential for criticism. She noticed, almost as an afterthought, that she was not anxious. Her body was calm. Her mind was clear. She participated without second-guessing herself.

Later, she realized something had changed during those six months. Not because she had been working on it, but because she had been living. The integration had happened beneath her awareness, in the ordinary moments of showing up to her life. The quiet had not been empty. It had been full of living.

Earlier in this process, moments of change may have been accompanied by recognition. You noticed patterns. Sensations stood out. Meaning emerged to organize experience. Over time, that quality softens. What once felt distinct becomes familiar. What once called for attention no longer does.

During these quieter stretches, the impulse to reflect fades. The process continues without being named. What you once held through conscious attention you now carry implicitly, shaping how you respond without requiring articulation.

Let the quiet exist. It belongs to the same unfolding. The relationship does not depend on activity or reflection. Even when the process grows still, engagement with life continues — unnamed, untracked, and real.

Being Affected

This process does not make life easier to absorb. Experience still lands with force. Loss still disrupts. Conflict still reorganizes the body. There are moments when what is happening exceeds what feels manageable, and the system responds by tightening, withdrawing, or reaching for control.

Earlier, you may have assumed that doing this work would soften life's impact — that greater awareness or capacity would mean less intensity, more steadiness, a kind of buffer between you and what happens. What becomes clearer is that the work does not reduce impact. It changes what you do with it.

Intensity does not have to register as failure. Reaction no longer needs defense or explanation. Experience can land without becoming evidence about who you are or what this work means.

I worked with someone whose father died suddenly. No warning, no time to prepare. One day he was there, the next he was not. She described the grief as total. It consumed her. She could not think straight. She could not function. She cried at random moments — in the grocery store, at her desk, in the car.

She said: I thought I'd be able to handle this better. I thought all the work I'd done would help me stay present with it, stay grounded. But I'm a mess. I can't hold anything.

What she was missing was that being a mess was staying present. The grief was moving through her without her trying to manage it or make it more palatable. She was not performing composure. She was not trying to be okay. She was letting herself be completely undone.

A few weeks later, she noticed something. The grief was still there, but she was not fighting it anymore. She was not trying to get through it or get over it. She was just in it. In the moments when the intensity eased, she could breathe. She could eat. She could sleep. The capacity to be affected had not made her immune to pain. It had made her able to let pain move through her without collapsing into a story about what it said about her strength or her progress.

When something hurts, it has reached you. When grief appears, it reflects connection. When fear or anger arises, life is pressing against something that matters. These responses do not need to be corrected before you can move forward.

There are moments when you lose orientation in the middle of impact — when attention is consumed by what is happening and any sense of ground feels distant. Orientation returns when it returns. Sometimes it shows up later, in how you speak, in what you choose next, in how the body settles. It was real even when it arrived late.

This process does not prevent collapse, confusion, or disorganization. What changes is how you hold those experiences. You stop taking them as interruptions to a stable self and recognize them as part of the movement of a life lived in contact.

Being affected was never the problem. The effort to avoid being affected was. As that effort loosens, life remains intense without threatening your relationship with yourself.

The Rhythm of Returning

Experience does not move in a straight line. It expands and contracts, opens and closes, widens and narrows. This is not something to correct. It is the ordinary rhythm of being human, living inside time, relationship, and change.

Contraction gets interpreted as regression — as if something has gone wrong, something has been lost. Expansion gets interpreted as arrival — as if you have finally reached the place you were trying to get to. Neither is true. Both are movements within a system that is continually adjusting to life.

Contraction as Return

When experience contracts — when awareness narrows, when familiar patterns return, when connection feels distant — the mind rushes to make sense of it. I am slipping backward. I am not doing the work. I am failing.

These conclusions form quickly. They offer a way to explain what is happening by turning it into a verdict about you.

Contraction does not mean you have regressed. It means conditions have shifted, and the system is responding as it knows how. Stress accumulates. Sleep changes. Relationships become tense. Demands increase. Loss arrives. The body is affected, and when it is, it reorganizes itself around what feels necessary. That reorganization often looks like protection — narrowing, withdrawal, familiar responses returning.

Nothing essential has disappeared. Wholeness has not gone anywhere. Capacity has not been lost. What shifts is access, and access moves with conditions. It always has.

Pause and Notice: Recognizing Contraction

Returning often happens before you recognize it. Attention narrows, familiar meanings organize quickly, and experience feels shaped by urgency, distance, or effort.

Notice how this shows up in your life right now. In recent days, have there been moments when experience felt tighter or more managed? When familiar reactions appeared quickly, or when connection to yourself or others felt less available?

Notice how you relate to those moments when they occur. Whether there is an impulse to correct, to interpret, to move yourself back toward openness. Or whether recognition happens more easily — an awareness that something has narrowed.

There is nothing here to change. This is noticing how returning is already moving within your experience.

Someone I worked with described a month when everything felt harder. She was more reactive with her partner, more anxious at work, slipping into patterns she thought she had moved past — overexplaining, people-pleasing, avoiding conflict. She said: I feel like I've lost everything I learned.

Nothing had been lost. She was moving through a period of contraction. Her nervous system was responding to a demanding season — her mother's health declining, a deadline at work, her daughter struggling at school. The conditions were heavy, and her system organized itself around getting through them.

When she stopped interpreting the contraction as failure, something became clearer. She was not regressing. She was responding. And the fact that she could recognize the patterns, even while they were happening, reflected a shift that had already taken place. The patterns were still there. Her relationship to them had changed.

Expansion as Return

If contraction is not failure, expansion is not success.

Expansion can feel like clarity, ease, a sense of being more yourself. Awareness feels closer. The body feels more familiar. Life feels more manageable. It is natural to interpret these periods as evidence that something has finally settled, that you have arrived somewhere you were trying to reach.

But expansion is not a destination. It is one expression of a larger rhythm. When contraction inevitably follows, the preceding expansion remains real. It means life has moved into a different configuration.

The difficulty begins when you treat expansion as something to maintain. Effort shifts to holding it in place, monitoring whether it is still present, trying to prevent the narrowing that will follow. Expansion becomes something to protect, and contraction becomes something to avoid. The work shifts from relationship to management.

When you stop treating expansion as proof, something eases. The body can rest in what feels open. Attention can soften without needing to confirm that contact is still there. You allow expansion to exist for as long as it does, and to recede when it does.

Pause and Notice: Recognizing Expansion

Just as experience narrows, it also widens again. Contact returns, often without effort and without warning.

Notice whether there have been times recently — even brief ones — when something felt more open after a period of contraction. Moments when your body felt more available, when attention settled without forcing it, when connection with others felt possible again.

These shifts happen on their own. They are not produced by effort, and they do not need to be maintained.

Notice what it is like to recognize access as it returns. Whether there is relief, hesitation, familiarity, or an impulse to hold onto it. Notice whether these moments are trusted, questioned, or quickly passed over.

There is nothing to preserve here. This is noticing how access already moves.

Someone once spoke about several months when she felt expansive. She was present with her children, clearer in her relationships, grounded in her body. I finally feel like myself, she said.

Then one morning she woke up and that feeling was gone. She felt distant, contracted, less clear. Her first reaction was panic. What happened? What did I do wrong? How do I get it back?

As she stayed with it, something became obvious. Nothing had happened. She had not done anything wrong. Life had shifted. The expansion had not been permanent, and it was never meant to be. It was one phase of movement, and now she was in another. Both belonged to the same process.

The Fluctuation Is the Process

Contraction and expansion are not separate experiences. They are movements within the same system. Life does not expand and remain expanded. It opens and closes, widens and narrows, in response to conditions that are always changing.

When expansion is present, contraction will eventually follow. When contraction is present, expansion will return. Neither lasts forever, and neither needs to. The process is not about eliminating one or maintaining the other. It is about staying in relationship with yourself as the fluctuation continues.

What matters is not the state. It is the contact within it.

Sometimes contact feels spacious. Sometimes it feels tight or distant. The contact itself carries continuity — not the quality of the experience.

The difficulty is rarely the fluctuation itself. It is the meaning that forms around it. When you interpret contraction as loss, it becomes harder to bear. When you interpret expansion as success, its ending feels like failure. When you recognize both as part of the same movement, the rhythm becomes easier to live inside.

Over time, expansion loses its status as proof, just as contraction loses its status as failure. Both become recognizable movements within a living system, adjusting to life as it unfolds. Wholeness was never located in expansion. It remains intact across both movements.

Returning Without Remembering

You will not always remember any of this when you need it.

You will not think: I should apply the principles. I should notice what phase I am in. You will just be in the middle of your life — the meeting, the argument, the ordinary Tuesday — and the work will either be there or it will not.

Return does not depend on recalling what this work has taught you. It arrives through the body before it arrives through language. You notice it in how your pace softens without intention, in the way your voice changes as bracing releases, in a decision that feels simpler than expected. Sometimes it appears as the relief of no longer pushing against what is happening.

There are periods when access fades so completely that even the sense of return feels absent. Experience organizes itself around what is required in the moment, and when conditions shift, orientation reappears without being summoned. It returns because the relationship has remained intact — not because you remembered anything.

Earlier in this process, remembering may have served as a bridge. A practice, a phrase, a familiar sensation helped reorient attention. That bridge becomes less necessary. Return begins to happen implicitly, shaped by experience rather than intention, with movement toward yourself occurring before you have named it.

Forgetting still happens. It just carries less meaning. Losing access no longer organizes experience around failure. It becomes one of many ways the system responds as life unfolds.

Return appears as the absence of struggle — when the body settles, urgency falls away, and something stops arguing with what is. This happens without requiring you to hold anything in mind. The process does not rely on recall. It unfolds because what you are in relationship with has always been closer than memory. Even when it goes unnoticed, the relationship continues, carrying you without requiring your participation.

I worked with someone who described realizing she had been moving differently for weeks before she noticed anything had shifted. She was not reflecting. She was not practicing. Life had been full — deadlines, a sick parent, ordinary exhaustion.

One afternoon, she declined an invitation without rehearsing an explanation, without the familiar spike of guilt. It was not empowering. It was unremarkable. Only later did she recognize that something had returned — a steadier way of staying with herself as decisions unfolded. She had not remembered anything she had learned. The relationship had simply resumed.

Sometimes returning happens without you noticing. You do not remember the principles. You do not reference the phases. You just live, and the living itself carries what has been learned.

Living Returning

At some point, the process stops being something you do and becomes something you live inside. You no longer organize attention around where you are within it. Life resumes its familiar complexity, and the phases recede from view. The work becomes invisible, which is how you know it has taken hold.

What becomes more noticeable is not the work itself but how access continues to move. There are moments when awareness feels close, and moments when attention narrows again. For a long time, the return to a familiar pattern felt like a verdict. It meant you were not trying hard enough, that you had lost your progress, that you were back at the beginning. To be in relationship with returning is to be freed from that interpretation. The return is just the return. It is the rhythm of being human. You forget, and then you remember. You lose the thread, and then you find it again.

In daily life, this may look like recognizing a familiar reaction sooner than before. Sensing when you are overwhelmed and need space. Moving through grief, stress, or change while still sensing that something steady remains underneath. At other times, you may feel fully pulled into old patterns. Both belong to the same process.

There is a trust in that rhythm, a confidence that is not about holding on, but about knowing you can always come back. The work is no longer about staying in a particular state. It is about living in the movement itself.

Nothing resolves permanently. Life continues to change, and you continue within it.

Ongoing Unbecoming

You will forget.

Not because something went wrong. Not because this was not real. But because you are human, and being human means that the conditioning runs deep, the patterns are familiar, and life keeps arriving with enough weight to pull attention back into old terrain.

You will become again. You will find yourself, at some point, back inside the story — the one about who you are, what you are capable of, what you need to be or do or fix before you can rest. It will feel true. It will feel like you. And for a while, you may not notice.

This is not failure. This is the human condition.

The nervous system does not abandon what it has practiced. Protection does not dissolve because you understand it. Meaning-making does not stop because you have seen through it. These are not flaws. They are features of being alive in a body that learned, long ago, how to survive.

And then one day — maybe gradually, maybe in a single moment — you will notice. You will recognize the tightness, the distance, the familiar effort of managing yourself through your own life. You will catch yourself mid-story.

That noticing is the return. You do not have to do anything with it. The orientation itself is the process — the same orientation that has been here from the beginning. The moment you recognize where you are, you are already back in relationship with yourself.

Unbecoming is not a destination you reach and hold. It is something that becomes available again and again, across a lifetime, in the ordinary moments of catching yourself. Each time you notice, you are already in it.

This is what it means to be human and to stay in relationship with yourself. Not to transcend the condition, but to remain inside it with a little more awareness, a little more ease. To forget and remember. To become and unbecome. To lose access and find it again — not because you are exceptional, but because you are willing to notice.

It does not end. It lives wherever you are, shaping how you meet the next moment, available again the instant you turn toward it.

And you will. That is the whole point.

Afterword

I did not write this from the outside. I am still inside the same movement this book describes. I lose access. I narrow. I forget. I return without knowing I am returning. I am affected by life in ways that surprise me, undo me, and ask something new of me each time.

I have edited this book more times than I can count. Each time, I returned to it convinced that something was unfinished — that a section needed more, that a concept was not quite landed, that the whole thing was not yet ready. I would revise, sit with it, feel better, and then return again with the same feeling. Something still undone. Something still not quite right.

At some point I had to sit with the possibility that this feeling was not a problem to solve. That the book would always feel a little undone, because that is what it is about. We have been so thoroughly trained to expect resolution — a clear conclusion, a final answer, a program with steps and outcomes and a bow on top. Something we can point to and say: there, it is finished, it worked. But that is not how this process moves, and it is not how being human actually works. Life does not resolve. It continues. And the work of staying with it, of returning to it without demanding that it finally make sense, is not a failure of the process. It is the process.

Writing this required stopping long enough to stay with experience without trying to make sense of it. I keep re-learning this, often subtly and often after the fact, rather than having mastered it.

If this book did anything, I hope it did not give you answers. I hope it gave you more room to stay with yourself when answers are not available. I hope it loosened the urgency to fix what is already moving.

I am not finished. Neither are you. That has never been the point.

I'll leave you here, where your life is already happening.

— Lacey

About the Author

Lacey K. Kelly is a licensed therapist, writer, and teacher whose work sits at the intersection of psychology, culture, and the question of what it means to be human when the old frameworks for meaning no longer hold. She writes and works in response to a particular kind of exhaustion — not just personal burnout, but the deeper, existential fatigue that comes from living inside systems that have asked us to optimize, perform, and endlessly improve ourselves into wholeness, while the ground beneath that project gives way.

Her clinical work draws from psychology, nervous system science, and lived experience to examine how awareness narrows under pressure, how protection forms in response to real conditions, and how change unfolds through relationship rather than force. Her approach does not center on fixing, optimizing, or transcending the self. Instead, it attends to what remains intact beneath adaptation — and how access to that ground becomes available as effort softens and contact deepens.

She is also the author of *God is a Dirty Word: A Cultural Reckoning with the God We Left Behind*, an exploration of how the language of the sacred has been flattened by culture and what gets lost when it is.

Lacey lives and works in Arizona, where she continues to write, teach, and practice alongside the questions that animate her work. Her ongoing work — essays, courses, conversations, and community — lives at theunbecomi nghub.com.

Continuing

If something in this book stayed with you, there is more.

At **theunbecominghub.com** you will find the full body of work this book belongs to — essays, a podcast, courses, and a community, all exploring the same territory from different angles.

The Writing — A weekly essay and podcast episode exploring what it means to step out of the endless project of becoming and return to being human. New pieces every week at theunbecominghub.com and on Substack.

The Books — *Already Human*, *The Process of Unbecoming*, and *God is a Dirty Word* each approach this work from a different direction. If you found your way here through one of them, the others are waiting.

The Courses — The Unbecoming Series offers a deeper, more structured exploration of the principles in this work — a way of staying in relationship with the process over time.

The Circle — A community space for people who want to continue this work in real time, with ongoing practices, reflections, and live support.

You can also find the podcast wherever you listen, and the weekly writing at Substack by searching *The Unbecoming Hub*.

To stay in touch and receive new essays directly:

theunbecominghub.com

Continuing

If something in this book stayed with you, there is more.

At **theunbecominghub.com** you will find the full body of work this book belongs to — essays, a podcast, courses, and a community, all exploring the same territory from different angles.

The Writing — A weekly essay and podcast episode exploring what it means to step out of the endless project of becoming and return to being human. New pieces every week at theunbecominghub.com and on Substack.

The Books — *Already Human*, *The Process of Unbecoming*, and *God is a Dirty Word* each approach this work from a different direction. If you found your way here through one of them, the others are waiting.

The Courses — The Unbecoming Series offers a deeper, more structured exploration of the principles in this work — a way of staying in relationship with the process over time.

The Circle — A community space for people who want to continue this work in real time, with ongoing practices, reflections, and live support.

You can also find the podcast wherever you listen, and the weekly writing at Substack by searching *The Unbecoming Hub*.

To stay in touch and receive new essays directly:

theunbecominghub.com

Returning to the Phases

T his section is not meant to be read straight through. It is a place to return to — when a phase feels close, when access has narrowed, when you want language to orient you without having to start from the beginning. Think of it less as the next chapter and more as a companion you can open anywhere.

Each section revisits one of the phases — not to move you forward, but to meet you where you already are.

It is tempting to want a final destination.

We are so trained to treat healing as a project that we naturally look for the finish line. We want a final resolution. We want to be done. We want to reach a point where all the questions are answered, the patterns are permanently broken, and the effort is finally over.

When the premise is that something is wrong with us, we interpret being back in a place we were before as failure. If we find ourselves tightening again, or reacting the way we used to, or losing access to the awareness we thought we had secured, we assume we have regressed. We assume there is more work to be done, another insight to uncover, another layer to fix.

But in the process of unbecoming, the return is not a regression. It is nature itself unfolding in its own rhythm.

The phases were never meant to happen once. They are not a sequence you graduate from. They continue to cycle, overlap, and reappear across time. Awareness moves into the foreground and then recedes. Patterns loosen and then reorganize under stress. Responsiveness becomes accessible and then tightens again when protection is needed. Aliveness expands and contracts as environments, relationships, and internal states shift.

None of this reflects failure. It reflects the ordinary movement of being alive.

When the ground changes, the meaning of this movement changes with it. Returning to a familiar phase is no longer a sign that you are broken; it is simply where you are. It is no longer work, because the effort has loosened. Returning is simply being human within the human condition as it unfolds.

This section exists as a place to return when access feels narrower, or when you want language to orient you again. Not to restart the process or move yourself forward, but to reconnect with what may already be present beneath the surface of experience.

Each chapter revisits one of the phases, offering additional reflections, common questions, and invitations to stay in relationship with what is unfolding in your life. The practices here are not meant to create change or produce a particular state. They are ways of bringing attention back into contact with experience as it already is.

Returning happens naturally. Sometimes it is gradual. Sometimes it happens in a single moment. Sometimes you recognize it only after it has already begun. This part of the book is simply a place to land when you want companionship in that movement.

Chapter 18

Awareness

I know I am back here when I catch myself running on automatic again — doing what I have always done, responding the way I was conditioned to respond, without any sense that I chose it. The filter is back. The old story is running. I am not living my life so much as executing it. I will be halfway through a conversation before I realize I have not actually been present for any of it. I have been performing a version of myself that formed a long time ago, in conditions that no longer exist.

When I notice that, I do not try to figure out how I got there. I just let the noticing be enough.

Conditioning does not disappear. It was never meant to. The patterns, assumptions, and automatic responses that formed through your early experiences were adaptations — ways your system learned to navigate the world you were given. They made sense then. They kept you safe, helped you belong, allowed you to function. The fact that they are still running is not a failure. It is what conditioning does. It persists.

What changes through this process is not the conditioning itself but your relationship to it. There are periods when that relationship feels spacious — when you can see the filter and choose whether to look through it. And there are periods when the filter closes back over experience and you are inside it again, without distance, without choice, without even noticing it has happened.

Returning to awareness here does not mean breaking free of conditioning. It means recognizing, again, that you are in it. That the story you are telling yourself about this moment, this person, this situation, was written a long time ago. That the response you are about to give was shaped by something that happened before you had language for it.

That recognition is not nothing. It is the whole thing.

You can return here whenever the filter feels thick again. Awareness does not require that conditioning stop. It only requires that you notice it is running.

Practices for the Return

Noticing the Filter

Conditioning operates as a filter — shaping what you perceive, what you expect, and how you interpret what happens around you. This practice invites you to notice the filter itself, not to remove it, but to recognize when experience is being organized by something older than this moment.

As you move through your day, notice moments when a response arrives before you have had time to think. A tightening in the chest when someone uses a certain tone. A familiar urge to explain yourself, to manage the room, to stay small, to take over. A story that forms instantly about what something means.

Pause when you notice one of these. Not to stop the response — it has already begun. Recognize: this came from somewhere. This is not just this moment. This is also every moment like it that came before.

What does it feel like to hold both at once — the present moment and the history it is activating? What is it like to notice the filter without needing to take it off?

When the Old Story Returns

There are particular stories that conditioning returns to most reliably. Stories about your worth, your capability, your safety, your belonging. Stories about what other people think, what you are allowed to want, what happens when you take up too much space.

When you notice one of these stories has returned, see if you can name it. Not analyze it, not trace it back to its origin, not decide whether it is true. Just name it.

There is the story that I am too much.

There is the story that I have to earn my place.

There is the story that something is wrong with me.

Notice what happens when the story is named rather than lived from. Notice whether any distance appears between you and it — even briefly, even slightly.

You are not trying to replace the story with a better one. You are noticing that it is a story. That it arrived. That it is not the same as the truth of this moment.

Recognition After the Fact

Awareness does not always arrive in the moment something happens. Often it appears later — after a conversation has ended, after a reaction has passed, or while moving through an ordinary task — when something from an earlier moment returns to mind.

At the end of the day, or at some quiet point after an interaction, allow one moment to come back into view. Something simple: a tightening during a conversation, a defensive reply, a sudden withdrawal, an impulse to explain or correct.

Notice that the moment is being remembered. Notice that awareness is present now, even if it was not accessible then.

There is no need to revisit the scene in detail or determine what it means. Register the sequence: conditioning activated, experience organized around it, and at some point recognition appeared. That recognition may have arrived seconds later or hours later. Its timing is not important. What matters is that awareness returns.

This practice builds familiarity with the way recognition unfolds. Awareness does not need to be immediate to be real. It arrives in its own time, and when it does, contact is restored.

What Tends to Arise Here

But isn't this just mindfulness?

It can look that way from the outside. Mindfulness is a practice of paying attention to the present moment without judgment. Awareness, as it is used here, is not a practice you do. It is a quality of your own nature that you return to. It is the part of you that was already watching, long before you learned any techniques. You do not have to cultivate it. You only have to notice that it is already here.

What if I notice, and then I just feel worse?

This is one of the most common and least-talked-about experiences of returning to awareness. You notice the tightness in your chest, and instead of it loosening, it gets louder. You notice the critical voice, and it gets more insistent. This is not a sign that you are doing it wrong. It is a sign that you are finally feeling the full weight of what has been there all along. The pain was always present. What is new is your attention to it. The work is not to fix the feeling, but to stay with the noticing — to let the awareness be a container for the discomfort, without needing it to change.

I have been in therapy for years. Why does this feel new?

Because therapy often works on the content — what happened, what it means, how to respond differently. Awareness, as a phase of the process, is not about the content. It is about the quality of your attention to your own experience. You may have spent years understanding your patterns without ever simply noticing them from the inside. Understanding and noticing are not the same thing. One is cognitive. The other is felt. This is the felt version.

What if I notice the same thing over and over and nothing changes?

The noticing is the change. Not in the sense that the pattern immediately dissolves, but in the sense that you are no longer fully inside it. There is now a small gap between you and the automatic response — a moment of awareness before the pattern runs. That gap is everything. It is where the rest of the process begins.

Chapter 19

Unraveling

I know I am back here when I lose the thread between me and the pattern. Not when I notice the pattern — that would be fine. But when I become it again. When the role is not something I am watching but something I am living from, without any distance, without any witness. I am the worry. I am the responsibility. I am the person who holds it all together, and that feels less like a choice and more like a fact. The fusion is the signal. When I cannot find the gap between what I am feeling and who I am, I know I am back in the middle of it.

Unraveling is fundamentally about relationship — the relationship between you and the patterns you have been living from. There are periods when that relationship has some space in it. You can see the role without being consumed by it. You can feel the pull of a familiar response without being fully carried by it. The pattern is present, but you are also present alongside it.

And then there are periods when that space closes. The pattern and the self collapse back together. You are not watching yourself accommodate — you are accommodating. You are not noticing yourself withdraw — you are gone. The fusion is not obvious. It is quiet. It is the feeling of being back inside a room you thought you had left, without remembering how you got there.

Returning to this phase is not about creating distance from yourself. It is about restoring the relationship. The gap between you and what you are experiencing — the small but essential space where choice lives — does not need to be wide. It only needs to exist.

When you find yourself fused again, the question is not what went wrong. The question is: can I be in relationship with this rather than identical to it? Can I notice what is happening without fixing it or explain it away?

That noticing is the unraveling. Not a dramatic dismantling, but a separation — the moment when the pattern becomes something you are having rather than something you are.

You can return here whenever the fusion feels complete again. The gap returns. It always does.

Practices for the Return

Noticing Identification

This practice invites you to notice moments when experience organizes itself around a role, belief, or familiar story — not to undo it, but to recognize it as something you are inhabiting rather than something you are.

Pause for a moment and notice what has been organizing your attention recently.

You might become aware of a familiar stance — being responsible, being careful, being capable, being quiet, being on guard, being needed, being invisible. Let one of these come into view, without deciding whether it is true or helpful.

Notice how it shows up. You may sense it in your body, in your posture, in the way your thoughts move, or in the way attention narrows.

There is nothing to change.

Notice what it is like to recognize this role or belief as something present, rather than something you must act from or resolve.

Stay with that noticing for a few breaths.

Pause and Notice: As attention rests, notice what is still here when the role is seen rather than inhabited. This may feel like space, steadiness, discomfort, neutrality, or nothing in particular. There is no expected experience. Identification may return immediately. That is not a problem. This practice does not remove identification. It introduces a moment of contact that does not require it.

When you are ready, let attention return to the body and the space around you.

If it feels natural, you might notice: What shifted when the role was recognized rather than enacted? What stayed the same? What was it like to not do anything with what you noticed?

When You Become the Pattern

There is a difference between noticing a pattern and being inside it. This practice is for the moments when you are already inside — when the fusion has happened and you are living from the role rather than watching it.

You may not recognize this while it is happening. You may only notice it afterward — when a conversation ends and you realize you had not been present in it, or when you catch yourself in the middle of a familiar loop and feel the slight vertigo of recognizing where you are.

When that recognition arrives, stay with it for a moment. Not to analyze how you got there or to judge yourself for being there. Just to register: I was fused. I am noticing now.

Notice what the fusion felt like from the inside. Was there urgency? A sense of necessity? A feeling that this was how things were, not a choice you were making? That quality — the sense of inevitability, of having no other option — is what fusion feels like. It is not a character flaw. It is what happens when a pattern is old enough and familiar enough that it stops feeling like a pattern and starts feeling like reality.

The noticing itself is the gap returning. You do not need to do anything else.

Meeting What Was Held

This practice invites contact with a younger aspect of yourself — not for healing or explanation, but to notice what becomes available when attention is offered without demand.

Parts of us form before language, meaning, or choice are available. They carry impressions of what it felt like to be small, dependent, uncertain, or alone. These are not stories you invented. They are traces of experience held in the body and nervous system, shaped by what was required at the time.

Find a place where your body can settle. Let your breathing move on its own.

When you are ready, allow a sense of a younger version of yourself to come into awareness. It may arrive as an image, a posture, a sensation, or a feeling. There is no need to search for a particular memory. What appears is enough.

Notice their quality — how they sit or move, the tone of their presence, the distance between you. Let attention remain uncomplicated. You are not required to feel warmth or connection. Staying present is sufficient.

You might imagine sitting nearby. Or holding them in awareness. If it feels natural, offer a simple acknowledgment: I see you. I'm here.

Let whatever arises — images, emotion, nothing at all — move without interpretation. Absence is also information.

When the contact feels complete, allow attention to return to your body and the room around you.

You do not need to draw conclusions. This is not about resolution. It is about contact.

Pause and Notice: Afterward, you may notice something subtle — a sensation that lingered, an impulse to fix, a pull to move away. Whatever appeared belongs to how experience once organized itself. Nothing here needs to be corrected. When you meet what was held early, something often becomes visible: the distance that formed around it. The tightening. The efficiency. The way experience learned to move quickly, stay small, stay strong, stay composed. Protection rarely forms without reason. It develops in proximity to something vulnerable.

Staying With Grief

Unraveling often surfaces grief — for what was needed but not received, for the ways you had to shape yourself to belong, for the energy spent holding things together. This is not a problem to be solved. It is a presence to be met.

When grief arises, see if you can notice it without understanding it. It may appear as sadness, but it may also show up as anger, numbness, or exhaustion. Notice where it lives in your body. Is there a weight, a hollowness, a tension? Let your attention rest there, without any agenda.

You do not need to make it move or release. You are offering it a place to be. If stories or memories arise, let them come and go without holding onto them. The grief is not in the story. It is in the body. Stay with the sensation, allowing it to be as it is, for as long as it needs.

What Tends to Arise Here

This just feels like I'm going backward. How is this progress?

It feels that way because the old structure is losing its integrity and the new one has not yet formed. You are in the in-between. Progress, in this phase, is not measured by feeling better. It is measured by your willingness to stay in the discomfort of not knowing, without rushing to fix it. The unraveling is the progress.

How long does this last?

There is no timeline. It lasts as long as it lasts. The attempt to measure it or hurry it along is the mind's desire for certainty — a subtle form of resistance to the phase itself. The only way through is to let go of the need for a map and trust that the ground is still there, even when you cannot feel it.

I feel like I am losing myself. Is that normal?

Yes. What you are losing is the version of yourself that was built on the old structure. The identity that organized itself around the pattern. That loss is real and it is worth grieving. But what is being lost is not you —

it is what you built to protect you. The essential nature underneath is intact. It was always intact. The unraveling is not destroying you. It is revealing you.

Should I be doing something? It feels like I should be doing something.

The impulse to act is the mind's attempt to regain control of a process that is not controlled by the mind. The most useful thing you can do in this phase is to stay with what is here, to let yourself be moved by it, and to resist the urge to fix, resolve, or accelerate. This is not passivity. It is a different kind of work — the work of staying present with what is uncomfortable, without turning away.

Chapter 20

Emerging

I know I am back here when choice disappears. Not dramatically — I am not incapacitated. But there is a familiar sense that I do not have options. That I have to respond this way, accommodate this person, take on this responsibility, stay quiet in this moment. The sense of agency that had been available goes offline, and what replaces it is the old feeling of being carried by circumstances rather than moving through them. I know something about myself that I cannot seem to access. The capacity is there. I just cannot reach it right now.

Emerging is about agency — the growing ability to act from your own values, needs, and limits rather than from conditioning. There are periods when that agency feels accessible. You speak up when something matters. You recognize a need and name it. You hold a boundary without collapsing or hardening. You make a choice that feels like yours.

And then there are periods when that access closes. The capacity does not disappear — it becomes unreachable. You know what you would say if you could say it. You know what you need but cannot bring yourself to ask for it. You find yourself accommodating again, deferring again, shrinking again, not because you decided to but because the alternative did not feel available.

This is what it feels like to return to this phase: not a loss of self, but a loss of reach. The self is there. The agency is there. The gap between knowing and doing has just widened again.

Returning here does not require forcing yourself to act differently. It involves staying in contact with what you know — what you value, what you need, where your edges are — even when acting from that knowledge feels out of reach. The contact itself keeps the capacity alive. It does not disappear when you cannot access it. It waits.

You can return here whenever agency feels distant. The capacity to act from yourself does not have to be exercised to remain real.

Practices for the Return

Sensing an Internal Compass

This practice attends to what becomes clearer when access to yourself is available. Values function as signals, registering when the nervous system is settled enough to stay with what is true without urgency. When access is present, they often appear through resonance rather than reasoning.

Begin by orienting your attention. You might pause for a few breaths or notice that you are here. Let that be enough.

Allow attention to move toward experiences that felt internally coherent. Moments where presence felt uncomplicated and where something essential was clear without explanation. This might have been a brief interaction, a choice that felt clean, or a moment of connection.

As these experiences come to mind, notice the qualities that were present. Stay with how experience was held. Let patterns form on their own.

Now notice what tends to feel meaningful, nourishing, or grounding. This may show up as a sense of rightness, as admiration for certain qualities in others, or as steadiness when those qualities are lived from.

As you sense these qualities, notice how your body responds. You may feel ease, clarity, warmth, or a subtle sense of alignment. At times, nothing distinct registers. That absence is part of how access moves.

If it feels natural, allow a few orienting qualities to be named. Keep them simple and provisional. Let them remain observations rather than commitments.

For each one, notice how alignment registers when it is present, how dissonance tends to show up when it is not, and what feels preserved or supported when you are in contact with it.

Stay with sensing rather than evaluation.

Values function as reference points that appear and recede as access allows. At times they shape perception or choice without warning. At other times, they remain in the background. When they are present, effort lessens as experience organizes with less internal friction.

Sensing What Is Needed

Notice what is already present in your body and attention. Sensation, fatigue, restlessness, emotional tone, or a general sense of strain may register first. Let experience come forward without shaping it.

As you stay with what is here, a sense of need may begin to surface. This might be physical, emotional, relational, or practical. It may appear clearly, or only as a faint pull toward rest, space, contact, or simplicity.

Stay with the felt quality of that need. Notice how it shows up — in the body, in mood, in pacing, in attention. Some needs register easily. Others carry hesitation, judgment, or a familiar urge to move past them. Let that be part of what you notice.

Patterns may come into view. Needs that tend to be postponed. Needs that were once unsafe to express. Needs that disappear when responsibility or urgency takes over. Nothing here requires explanation.

If writing is available, let a few words form that name what you notice. Not to decide what to do, but to stay close to what is present. Which needs feel near? Which feel distant? Which feel familiar?

Needs register information about what supports capacity, integrity, and aliveness. When they are sensed clearly, agency sometimes organizes without deliberation. Direction emerges through contact rather than effort.

Sensing the Edge

Boundaries come into view when values and needs are felt clearly. They arise as an edge — the place where inner orientation meets outer demand. This practice stays with that edge as it registers, without shaping it or arguing with it.

When the edge is present, experience holds together. Engagement feels possible without strain. When it blurs, signs often appear: fatigue, resentment, tension, withdrawal. These signals point toward a boundary already forming.

Begin by returning to what you have already noticed about what matters and what supports you. Let that orientation remain in the background.

Bring attention to areas of your life where energy thins or effort increases. Places where you feel pulled past yourself, braced, diminished, or resistant. Let one situation come into focus.

Stay with the felt sense of that situation. Notice what value feels touched there. Notice what need is asking for recognition. Let the boundary begin to show itself through sensation, impulse, or clarity rather than language.

If words form, allow a simple statement to arise — not as a declaration, but as a description of what is already present. Something like: This is as far as I can go. This is what I can offer. This needs to stop here.

Remain with what follows. Notice what this boundary holds in place. Notice how your body responds when the edge is acknowledged. Notice whether an action appears naturally, without planning or explanation.

Let the boundary stand without rehearsing how it will be communicated or received.

Notice what it is like to recognize a boundary without moving away from yourself. Where do edges feel familiar or steady? Where do they feel fragile or newly visible? What part of you anticipates discomfort, tension, or loss when an edge is honored? What helps you stay present there without collapsing or hardening? Boundaries arise through contact, not control. They do not require force to exist. They allow you to remain in relationship with yourself while staying in relationship with the world. They do not push others away. They mark where you remain.

What Tends to Arise Here

Is this when I finally start doing the work?

It can feel that way, because this is often the first time that a sense of agency returns. But the work is not about making things happen. It is about noticing the impulse to move, and following it. The energy for the movement comes from the ground of wholeness, not from your will. Your work is to notice the subtle impulse and not get in its way.

What if I don't feel any new impulses? What if I just feel empty?

Emptiness is not a sign of absence. It is a sign of space. After the density of the unraveling, the quiet can feel like nothing is happening. But this is the space from which the new thing will emerge. The invitation is to rest in the emptiness, to let it be, without needing to fill it with activity or meaning. The impulse will come when it is ready.

I feel hopeful, but I am scared to trust it. What if I crash again?

That fear is understandable, and it is worth naming. You have been through enough cycles to know that the good feeling does not always last. But the fear of the next unraveling is not a reason to hold back from the emerging. The emerging is not a promise that nothing hard will happen again. It is an invitation to be fully here, in this moment of opening, without needing to protect yourself from the next one. The ground will hold you then, as it is holding you now.

The changes I am making feel small. Am I doing enough?

Small is exactly right. Emerging does not announce itself. It does not look like a dramatic reinvention. It looks like a slightly different response in a familiar situation. It looks like saying yes to something you would have avoided. It looks like a moment of rest that does not feel like failure.

The smallness is not a sign of insufficient effort. It is the nature of the phase.

Chapter 21

Animating

I know I am back here when life stops feeling like enough. Not because anything is wrong exactly — I can point to evidence that things are fine. But there is a withdrawal happening, a pulling back from the texture of ordinary experience. Food tastes like food, but not quite. Conversations happen but do not land. I move through my days, and nothing accumulates into anything. It is not depression. It is more like a glass wall between me and my own life. I am present but not participating. I am here but not in it.

For me, this shows up as going flat — not sadness exactly, not anxiety, just a numbing out. I will realize I have been moving through my days functionally, getting everything done, but not actually in any of it. The color drains out. My old habit was to force energy back — push harder, exercise more, manufacture some kind of spark. Now I know the flatness is just my system conserving what it has. The way back is not forcing aliveness. It is letting myself be exactly as tired or as flat as I actually am.

Animating is about participation — the capacity to be genuinely present in your own life, to let experience actually land, to be moved by what is moving and still by what is still. There are periods when this capacity is available. You are in the conversation, not just conducting it. You taste the food. You feel the warmth of a particular afternoon. Ordinary life has texture and weight.

And then there are periods when participation withdraws. The system pulls back from contact. Not dramatically — you are still functioning, still showing up, still doing what needs to be done. But something essential is behind glass. You are watching your life from a slight remove.

This withdrawal is not a failure of aliveness. It is the system protecting itself. When demands have been high, when resources have been low, when contact has felt too risky or too costly, the nervous system conserves by reducing participation. It is the same intelligence that formed your early adaptations, doing what it knows how to do.

Returning to this phase does not require generating enthusiasm or forcing yourself back into contact. It involves allowing the withdrawal to be what it is — a signal, not a verdict — and staying close enough to ordinary experience that participation can return on its own when the system is ready.

Life does not need to feel extraordinary for you to be in it. It only needs to be enough. And when the glass wall is up, the practice is to stay near the glass, without demanding that it come down.

Practices for the Return

Staying With Response

At times, response is already underway before there is space to decide what to do. Tension, urgency, withdrawal, or impulse may appear in the middle of a conversation, while making a choice, or during an otherwise unremarkable moment.

When this happens, experience can be allowed to continue without being redirected. Response does not need to be acted on immediately, explained, or resolved. Remaining with it long enough for it to move on its own is often enough.

Notice what is happening in the body right now. There may be a sense of pulling back, of flatness, of distance from what is around you. Let that be present without trying to change it.

If there is a quality to the withdrawal — fatigue, a kind of heaviness, a sense of going through the motions — stay with that quality. Not to analyze it or fix it. Just to be in contact with it.

Sometimes the simple act of noticing the withdrawal softens it. Not always. But the noticing itself is a form of participation — a way of being in relationship with your own experience even when experience feels thin.

Noticing the Ordinary

Participation does not require peak experiences. It lives in the small, unremarkable moments of ordinary life. This practice invites you to stay with one ordinary moment long enough to let it register.

Choose something simple. A cup of something warm. The quality of light in the room. The sound of something nearby. A brief exchange with another person. Something that is already present and requires nothing of you.

Bring your attention to it fully, for just a few moments. Not to manufacture appreciation or force presence. Let the ordinary thing be what it is, and to notice whether anything in you meets it.

You may notice nothing. The glass wall may stay up. That is fine. You were still there, still close enough to notice.

This practice builds familiarity with the texture of ordinary experience — not as something to be grateful for or savored, but as the actual substance of a life being lived.

When Life Feels Like It Should Be More

There is a quality to this phase that can feel like an existential ache — a sense that life should feel different than it does, that you should be more engaged, more present, more alive. That something is missing.

When this feeling arrives, see if you can notice it without immediately trying to resolve it. The ache is not evidence that something is wrong. It is what happens when the system is between states — when the old ways of generating meaning through effort and achievement have loosened, and the new way of finding meaning in ordinary presence has not yet fully settled.

You are not failing to be alive. You are in the gap between one way of being and another.

Stay with the ache for a moment. Notice where it lives in your body. Notice whether it carries urgency or a kind of weight. Notice whether the impulse to fix it arises, and what it would want to fix.

You do not need to resolve this. The ache is part of the transition. It does not mean life is not enough. It means you are still learning to let it be.

Notice what ordinary participation actually feels like when it is present — not the dramatic moments, but the small ones. The moment a conversation actually landed. The moment you tasted something and it registered. The moment you felt your own feet on the floor. These moments are not lesser than the ones you are waiting for. They are the substance of what you are returning to.

What Tends to Arise Here

Sometimes this phase feels expansive and alive. Other times it feels like nothing at all. How do I hold onto the good parts?

You don't. The attempt to hold on is the mind trying to turn a state into a trait — to capture the aliveness and put it in a jar. Animation is not a reward for good behavior, and it is not a permanent state of feeling good. It is the capacity to participate more fully in your life as it is. Sometimes that will feel expansive. Sometimes it will feel quiet, or difficult, or ordinary. The work is not to curate a particular feeling, but to inhabit your life as it unfolds, trusting that the ground remains even when the feeling of aliveness recedes.

What if my life doesn't look different? My circumstances are the same, but I'm told I should be changing.

Animation is an internal shift before it is an external one. The first change is not in what you are doing, but in how you are being in the doing. You might be doing the same job, living in the same house, having the same conversations — but you are present in them in a way you were not before. The pressure to perform a visible transformation for others is part of the old paradigm. The real shift has already happened. The external changes will come on their own, or they won't.

I feel more sensitive than before, and it's not always comfortable. Is this progress?

It is. For a long time, much of your energy was invested in holding yourself together, managing your experience, and maintaining a certain identity. As that effort loosens, the armor thins. The result is not always a feeling of expansive joy. It is often a period of increased sensitivity. You feel more — not just more joy or aliveness, but also more grief, more irritation, more of the un-lived life that was waiting underneath the protection. This is not a sign that something is wrong. It is a sign that your capacity to feel is returning. The stability will grow alongside the sensitivity, but it often arrives later.

I still feel like I'm getting it wrong. I have moments of presence, and then I'm right back in the old patterns.

The idea that you could get this wrong belongs to the becoming paradigm. There is no "further along" to get to, and no state to achieve and then lose. There is only the rhythm of being human. You will have moments of clarity, and you will have moments of being completely caught. You will feel free, and you will feel the old constraints tighten around you again. The process does not have a finish line. It has a rhythm. You are in the rhythm. That is enough.

Chapter 22

Returning

I still lose my footing. I still get caught in old stories about my worth, still tighten up when I feel misunderstood, and still have days where the premise that something is wrong with me feels like an absolute fact. The difference now is not that I don't leave. The difference is that I know how to come back. I don't beat myself up for forgetting anymore. I just recognize the forgetting as part of the rhythm.

Returning is about the forgetting. Not as a failure, not as a relapse, but as the most human thing there is. You will forget. You will drift back into the conditioning, back into the fusion, back into the sense that you have no options, back into the glass wall between you and your own life. You will lose the thread. You will wake up one day and realize you have been gone for a while — a week, a month, longer — and you will not be entirely sure when it happened.

This is not a sign that the process failed. It is the process. The forgetting is built into being human. We are not designed for permanent arrival. We are designed for return.

What changes is not that the forgetting stops. What changes is what happens when you notice it. The old response to forgetting was to make it mean something — to turn it into evidence that you were broken, that you had not done enough, that you would never really change. The new response is simpler. You notice. You are back. That is the whole thing.

The noticing is the return. You do not have to do anything else. You do not have to restart, retrace your steps, or work your way back through everything you have learned. The moment you recognize that you have been gone is the moment you are already here again.

You can return here whenever the forgetting has happened. Nothing was lost while you were away. The capacity to return is not something you can misplace. It is part of what you are.

Practices for the Return

Recognizing the Forgetting

Forgetting does not always arrive. It tends to happen gradually, in the background of a life that is busy with other things. You may not notice it until you are already well inside it.

This practice invites you to recognize the signs of forgetting — not to prevent it, but to become familiar with how it moves in you specifically.

Look back over the past few weeks. Notice whether there have been periods where you felt more automatic, more reactive, more carried by circumstances than choosing within them. Periods where the old stories felt more like facts. Periods where you were functioning but not quite present.

If you find one of those periods, stay with it for a moment. Not to analyze it or trace it back to a cause. Just recognize: I was gone for a while there.

Notice what it feels like to recognize that now. Notice whether judgment arises — the impulse to make the forgetting mean something about you. See if you can let the forgetting be what it was: a period of forgetting. Human. Ordinary. Already over.

When the Old Stories Feel Like Facts

There are particular stories that return most reliably when you have forgotten. Stories about your worth, your belonging, your capability, your safety. Stories that feel, when you are inside them, less like stories and more like the truth of things.

When you notice one of these stories running, see if you can name it without arguing with it.

There is the story that I am not enough.

There is the story that I have to earn my place.

There is the story that something is fundamentally wrong with me.

The naming is not a technique for making the story go away. It is the act of recognizing that it is a story — that it arrived, that it has been here before, and that it will pass.

You do not need to replace it with a better story. You do not need to convince yourself it is not true. You only need to notice that you are having it, not it.

That noticing is the return.

Staying With Nothing Happening

The process of unbecoming is not always marked by insight or intensity. There are periods where it feels like nothing is happening. The landscape is flat. The process feels distant. This is not a sign that you are stuck. It is a different kind of territory.

When you find yourself in one of these periods, see if you can resist the urge to make something happen. Notice the pull to find a new problem, to seek a new insight, or to question whether you are doing it wrong. Let your attention rest in the ordinariness of it all. The quiet. The flatness. The absence of charge.

What is it like to stay here, without needing it to be different? What happens when you let this moment be exactly as it is, without demanding that it offer you anything more?

What Tends to Arise Here

So the process just starts over? What was the point of all that work?

The point was not to arrive at a destination where you never have to do the work again. The point was to learn the rhythm of the work itself. Returning is not a failure. It is the final phase of the process — the one that reminds you that this is a spiral, not a line. You are not starting over. You are returning to the same ground, but with a different kind of attention, and a deeper trust in your own capacity to be with what is here.

Does it get easier?

Yes and no. The circumstances of your life will continue to be as difficult and as beautiful as they have always been. What gets easier is your relationship to them. The gap between forgetting and remembering gets shorter. The trust in your own capacity deepens. The need to fix or manage or understand gives way to a willingness to just be here, in the midst of it all.

I feel like I have lost all the progress I made. How do I find my way back?

You are already on your way back. The noticing that you have drifted is the returning. It is not a separate step that comes after the awareness — it is the awareness itself. You have not lost the ground. You have temporarily lost your attention to it. The ground is where it has always been. You are standing on it now, even as you read this.

I am tired of the cycle. I just want to be done.

That exhaustion is real and worth honoring. The desire to be done is the desire for a life without difficulty, without the recurring invitation to return to yourself. That life is not available. But what is available is a different relation-ship to the cycle — one in which the returning feels less like failure and more like familiarity. The cycle does not end. But the way you move through it changes, and does change, with each pass through.

www.ingramcontent.com/pod-product-compliance
Lightning Source LLC
Chambersburg PA
CBHW020336180726
47991CB00020B/1723